French Moderist Library

SERIES EDITORS

MARY ANN CAWS

RICHARD HOWARD

PATRICIA TERRY

THE CUBIST POETS IN PARIS

THE CUBIST POETS

IN PARIS

AN ANTHOLOGY

University of Nebraska Press: Lincoln and London

EDITED BY L. C. BREUNIG

© 1995 by the University of Nebraska Press. All rights reserved. Manufactured in the United States of America. The paper in this book meets the minimum requirements of American National Standard for Information Sciences—Permanence of Paper for Printed Library Materials, ANSI z39.48-1984. Text set in 10.5 on 15 pt Berthold Bodoni by Keystone Typesetting Co. Printed by Bookcrafters. Designed by R. H. Eckersley. Frontispiece: *Le livre*, by Serge Férat. © 1991, ARS NY / ADAGP   Library of Congress Cataloging in Publication Data. The Cubist poets in Paris : an anthology / edited by L.C. Breunig.   p.   cm.—(French modernist library) Includes bibliographical references and index. ISBN 0-8032-1224-0   1. French poetry—20th century—Translations into English. 2. French poetry —20th century.   3. Cubism—France—Paris. 4. Cubism—Poetry.   1. Breunig, LeRoy C., 1915-. 11. Series. PQ1170.E6C78 1995 841′.91208—dc20 94-9379 CIP

One can only marvel at the instinct of Parisian

painters to keep their art in the hands of poets. — ROBERT MOTHERWELL

To Alexandra Daphne

CONTENTS

List of Illustrations   ix

Acknowledgments   xi

Introduction   xiii

1. Pierre Albert-Birot   1

2. Guillaume Apollinaire   23

3. Blaise Cendrars   81

4. Jean Cocteau   111

5. Sonia Delaunay   133

6. Paul Dermée   143

7. Pierre Drieu La Rochelle   161

8. Charlotte Gardelle   173

9. Vicente Huidobro   179

10. Max Jacob   199

11. Marie Laurencin   229

12. Hélène d'Oettingen   239

13. Raymond Radiguet   255

14. Pierre Reverdy   269

15. André Salmon   287

Selected Bibliography   309

Index   317

ILLUSTRATIONS

Le Livre, Serge Férat — Frontis

1. *La Cartelettre*, Juan Gris — xx
2. *La Montre*, Juan Gris — xxii
3. *Les Voyelles de Rimbaud*, Robert Delaunay — xxvi
4. *Apollinaire*, Orfeo Tamburi — 68
5. *Jean Cocteau*, self-portrait — 128
6. *Zenith*, Sonia Delaunay and Blaise Cendrars — 140
7. *Paul Dermée*, Pierre Gallien — 156
8. *Papier collé*, Paul Dermée and Juan Gris — 158
9. *Group of Artists*, Marie Laurencin — 234
10. *The Baroness d'Oettingen with friends*, Giorgio de Chirico — 248
11. *L'homme glisse . . .*, Léopold Survage — 250
12. *Baroness d'Oettingen*, Léopold Survage — 252
13. *Pierre Reverdy*, Juan Gris — 282
14. *Sailor in a Bar*, Louis Marcoussis — 304
15. *André Salmon*, Moïse Kissling — 306

ACKNOWLEDGMENTS

Grateful acknowledgment is made to the following for permission to reprint previously printed material: Rare Book and Manuscript Library, Columbia University, for Apollinaire's *En forme de cheval*, *Jet d'eau*, and *Vase*, all from *Calligrammes*; Editions Denoël for excerpts from Cendrars's *Poésies complètes*; Editions Flammarion for excerpts from Reverdy's *Le Gant de crin* and *Poésie*; Pierre Cailler for excerpts from Laurencin's *Le Carnet des nuits*; Editions Gallimard for excerpts from Albert-Birot's *Poésie*, Apollinaire's *Oeuvres poétiques*, Cocteau's *Poésies*, Drieu La Rochelle's *Écrits de jeunesse*, Jacob's *Le Cornet à dés* and *Laboratoire central*, and Salmon's *Carreaux*; Vicente Huidobro for excerpts from his *Obras completas*; and Jean-Michel Place for reproduction of Dermée's poems from *Nord-Sud* and *SIC*, of Gardelle's poems from *SIC*, of Baroness d'Oettingen's poems from *Nord-Sud*, and of Radiguet's poems from *SIC*.

I also wish to acknowledge Editions Gallimard for permission to translate Apollinaire's 'Zone' from *Alcools* and 'Les Fenêtres' from *Calligrammes*.

My many thanks to Liliane Ziegel (Mrs. Olivier Ziegel) for the inexhaustible help she gave me through the years, without which this work could hardly be completed.

To Polly Rimer Duke, my gratitude for editing and correcting the proofs, thus putting the final touches on this book.

I thank Mary Missirian for her patience in typing the manuscript.

From the moment of its inception in the first decade of the twentieth century cubism has had to come to terms with its literary counterpart. Pierre Reverdy, like other poets, considered the term 'cubist poetry' an absurdity. Yet today, with cubism itself taking its position as the seminal movement in the art of the century, the dozen or so French poets who surrounded Picasso and his circle in Paris on the eve of and during the First World War have become an integral part of the school. Recent exhibits, reprints, and monographs have revealed a much greater degree of collaboration between the cubist painters and poets than had been suspected. Blaise Cendrars set forth the relationship between poets and painters, placing himself with Delaunay and Léger, Reverdy with Braque, Max Jacob with Picasso, and Apollinaire with 'everybody.'

Who were these poets? The language barrier has prevented many of them from crossing the Channel or the Atlantic, and it is to acquaint English-speaking audiences with their works that I present this bilingual anthology. (Unless otherwise noted, translations are my own.) If I omit Gertrude Stein, William Carlos Williams, e. e. cummings, and their compatriots, it is because I am limiting myself to the Francophones.

The cubist poets were a rather motley group of diverse origins, including a number of foreigners, whom the French chauvinists disdainfully called *métèques*. They were united among themselves and with the painters in their rejection of what Ezra Pound called the 'talcum powder' poetry of the nineties, their salute to the new century, their love of innovation, and their search for a language that would bring poetry and the arts ever closer.

In alphabetical order, we meet Pierre Albert-Birot, conceived in Algeria, born in Angoulême, painter, sculptor, poet, and founder of the cubist review *SIC* (for *sons, idées,* and *couleurs*); Guillaume Apollinaire, half Polish, born in Rome, raised on the Côte d'Azur, acknowledged leader of the cube and other isms, founder of *Les Soirées de Paris,* a major poet of the twentieth century; Blaise Cendrars, Swiss-born chain-smoking globetrotter; Jean Cocteau (plural, he says, of *cocktail*), the chic of the avant-garde; Sonia Delaunay, from the Ukraine, poet, painter, designer, simultanist; Paul Dermée, Belgian-born poet-philosopher, number-two man of the review *Nord-Sud;* Pierre Drieu La Rochelle, collaborator with *SIC,* more Claudelian than cubist; Charlotte Gardelle, Rumanian-born member of the Salon d'Automne; Vicente Huidobro, from Santiago de Chile, Francophone and Francophile; Max Jacob, discoverer of Picasso, convert to Catholicism, logomaniac; Marie Laurencin, the muse in Le Douanier Rousseau's *Muse Inspiring the Poet;* the Baroness Hélène d'Oettingen, whose pseudonym changed with each genre; Raymond Radiguet, child prodigy who died at twenty after publishing cubist poems and two major novels; Pierre Reverdy, the purist, founder of *Nord-Sud,* named for the Métro line that connects Montmartre and Montparnasse; and André Salmon, who with Picasso, Max Jacob, and Apollinaire formed the nucleus of the movement in the studios of the Bateau-Lavoir on Montmartre.

Before we see how these poets fit in, let us take a look at the word 'cubism.' Is 'cubist painting' any less absurd than 'cubist poetry'? It is true that there are cubes in a few of the early paintings of Braque and Picasso, enough to have prompted the remark, 'Look at all the little cubes!' attributed to Matisse and taken up by the critic Vauxcelles, but hardly enough to have inspired the name of a rich new ism. The word must have taken on connotations as its usage developed. Its brevity and its concreteness were in part responsible for its success. Where other isms because of their abstractness fell by the wayside—Albert-Birot's nunism, Huidobro's creationism, even Romain's unanimism—the word 'cubism' lent itself to any number of associations.

A certain lighthearted playfulness accompanies it. Apollinaire connects it with KUB, the bouillon cube, in an anecdote according to which Matisse, on arriving in Collioure for the summer season in 1911, was chagrined to find on a wall of his house the three letters on a huge poster; the wall, it seems, had been let out to an advertising firm. In 1912 Picasso painted two still lifes that contained the same three letters. On one of the canvases he painted a transparent cube of the kind that every school boy and girl draws, with the optical illusion caused by the shifting planes and symbolizing, if you will, the use of ambiguity as a cubist device. Meanwhile, Cendrars, not to be outdone, discovered another bouillon, newly imported from Germany, called OXO. When Max Jacob chose the title *Le Cornet à dés* (The dice shaker) for a volume of his prose poems, he was certainly aware that the Greek word for a die is κυβος (cube). Mallarmé's famous title 'Un Coup de dés . . . ' (A dice throw) could have read 'Un Coup de cube . . . ' (A cube throw). Here again Picasso vies with the poets when he reduces the newspaper headline 'Un Coup de Théâtre' (Theatrical play), something to do with the Balkan Wars, to 'Un Coup de Thé.' Poet and painter alike will stop at nothing in their wordplay. Meanwhile, the conservative press invariably spells 'cubism' with a *k* to underline its supposedly alien origins. Today the aptness of the word is no longer questioned: it is accepted as a most felicitous term, elastic enough to stretch from babies' alphabet blocks to the 'apprehension of the essential qualities of dice cubes by Edmund Husserl.'[1]

In what ways did these poets express their entente? We can discern three in particular: as art critics defending the new painting, as collaborators providing the text for illustrations, and as poets in their own right using techniques borrowed from or exchanged with the painters. Among the handful of art critics sympathetic to cubism before the First World War, the best known were Apollinaire and Salmon, who had art columns in the Parisian press. Louis Vauxcelles, who was not sympathetic to cubism, nevertheless eulogized those whom he called 'poet-critics,' including Apollinaire and Salmon. We may extend the term to cover almost all the major poets in this volume, although their critical writing was somewhat scattered. Limiting ourselves to a sampling of remarks on Picasso, we see how each writer found for the same subject his own poetic style. Salmon, for whom the anecdote was a way of reaching a truth, related in *La Jeune Peinture française* (Recent French painting) how Picasso by the

1. See Edward F. Fry, *Cubism* (New York: McGraw Hill, 1966), 39.

mere addition of a crown of roses, a 'sublime stroke of caprice,' changed a painting into a masterpiece.[2] Max Jacob, usually so whimsical and so given to wordplay, became deadly serious when he called Picasso an 'abyss,' adding: 'He does not exist, he creates himself, as Vico said of God.'[3] Apollinaire, who loved to make aphorisms out of similes and metaphors, wrote in *Les Peintres cubistes* (Cubist painters) the open-ended line, 'A man like Picasso studies an object as a surgeon dissects a corpse.'[4] Cendrars, who relished enumerations, wrote in *Aujourd'hui* (1919): 'The painter cuts, pierces, saws, stabs, draws and quarters, rips, strangles. Suddenly matter is there. Before your eyes. Perceptibly larger.'[5] Reverdy, who generally preferred the painting to the painter, wrote less of Picasso than of cubism itself: 'The public demands that a work transport it elsewhere, whereas cubism claims to fix the reader's mind on the work as with a pin.'[6] Add to Picasso's the names of the other cubist painters, and you will invariably find a poet to appreciate them.

More revealing than critical appreciation, however, is actual collaboration, for which we have a considerably longer list than the one drawn up by Cendrars. Salmon and Cocteau both collaborated with Picasso; Dermée with Marcoussis and Laurens; Jacob with Gris; Oettingen with Survage, Allard Laboureur, and Justman Orloff; and Apollinaire with Derain, Survage, Gris, and Férat. And all this within the cubist ranks. The works, for the most part prints resulting from the collaborations, came to be known as *livres de peintres* or *livres d'artistes*, largely because the painters, unlike most nineteenth-century painters (with the notable exception

2. Ibid., 81.

3. Max Jacob to Jean Cocteau, 1926, cited in L. C. Breunig, 'Max Jacob et Picasso,' *Mercure de France* 131 (1957), 581–96.

4. In *Oeuvres complètes de Guillaume Apollinaire*, ed. Michel Décaudin, 4 vols. (Paris: Balland et Lecat, 1966), 1:19 (translation mine).

5. In Blaise Cendrars, *Selected Writings*, ed. Walter Albert (New York: New Directions, 1966), 233–34; see also the translator's list there.

6. *Le Gant de crin* (Paris: Librairie Plon, 1926), 25 (translation mine).

of Manet and Mallarmé), were closely involved with the poets in the production of the works.

The person who was mainly responsible for launching the *livres de peintres*, cubist and otherwise, was the art dealer D. H. Kahnweiler, the son of a Stuttgart banker, who moved to Paris in his twenties and befriended both the poets and the painters of the Bateau-Lavoir. In 1909 he offered to publish Apollinaire's medieval fantasy on the Merlin theme, *L'Enchanteur pourrissant* (The rotting magician). Apollinaire and Kahnweiler agreed on the painter André Derain, whom Apollinaire at that time esteemed as one of the founders of cubism, as the illustrator. Derain did a series of highly schematized woodcuts depicting the various characters along with the flora and fauna that harmonized with the printed pages of the text.

Kahnweiler turned next to Max Jacob, who with some trepidation allowed Picasso to do the etchings for the first and third volumes (1911 and 1914) of his *Saint Matorel* trilogy, which relates the conversion and eventual canonization of a pathetic young Parisian worker who is obviously Jacob's alter ego. If Jacob was worried, it was simply that he feared Picasso's mockery. Actually one senses that Picasso was somewhat more involved in solving the problems of perspective and volume than in portraying the characters. The cover of *Saint Matorel* was the first to carry Kahnweiler's monogram, the initials *H.K.* (Henry Kahnweiler) with a seashell motif on either side. Apollinaire had apparently quoted the adage that no editor can allow more than two *coquilles*, meaning both 'seashell' and 'printer's error.'

Max Jacob was paired with Juan Gris in the first work to be published by Kahnweiler after the war, *Ne coupez pas Mademoiselle ou Les Erreurs des P.T.T.* (1921). By omitting the comma (like all good cubists since Apollinaire's deletion of punctuation in *Alcools*), Jacob transformed the set phrase in the title, *Ne coupez pas Mademoiselle*, or 'Don't cut me off, operator,' to 'Don't cut up the young lady.' This allowed Jacob both to cite various bizarre telephone messages and wrong numbers and to create a good-natured giant who tries to prevent the damsel from being butchered. Gris caught the spirit of Jacob's whimsy both in his choice of subject and in the execution of the four lithographs that accompany the text. The print with the letters spelling CARTELETTRE (letter-card) is based on some verbal acrobatics going from *tourtelette* to *tartelettre* to *cartelettre* (see plate 1). Gris undoubtedly saw the graphic effects to be obtained from the compound word that he associated at the same time with the postal service, P.T.T. (Post, Telephone, and Telegraph Offices).

Another lithograph, showing a telephone linesman protecting a little girl, bears the name ALCOFIBRAS in large capital letters. He is our giant of course, since he must be as good-natured as those portrayed by ALCOFIBRAS NASIER, the pseudonymic anagram of FRANÇOIS RABELAIS.

Kahnweiler remained quite faithful to the cubist style in the *livres de peintres* that he produced in the twenties. These include Malraux and Léger's *Lunes en papier* (Paper moons), Radiguet and Laurens's *Les Pélicans*, Satie and Braque's *Le Piège de Méduse* (Medusa's trap), Reverdy and Manolo's *Coeur de chêne* (Heart of oak), Radiguet and Gris's

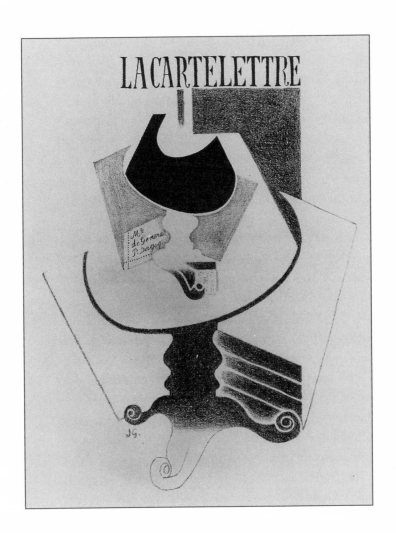

Denise, and Gertrude Stein and Gris's *A Book Concluding With as a Wife Has a Cow.*

Among the cubist painters, Gris and Marcoussis were particularly sensitive to the poetry they illustrated. In one of Gris's works the text of a poem by Paul Dermée is actually incorporated as a collage. In Gris's oil plus collage entitled *La Montre* (The watch) (see plate 2) one sees on the right the title LE PONT MIRABEAU (Mirabeau Bridge), which serves as both homage to its author, Apollinaire, and as a link between the watch in the painting and the passage of time, which is the poem's theme. A connection is also established between the word *boire* (drink) from Apollinaire's sonnet 'L'Enfer' (Hell) and the bottle of sherry in Gris's composition.

The most ambitious *livre de peintre* among the cubists was undoubtedly Marcoussis's series of thirty-four etchings for *Alcools*. The portrait of Apollinaire completed before *Alcools* was published bears the original title of the volume, *Eau-de-Vie*. Like Gris, Marcoussis inserted along with other titles from Apollinaire a text from the poet's own work. At the bottom of the portrait there is an excerpt from the poem 'Cortège':

> Un jour
> Un jour je m'attendais moi-même
> Je me disais Guillaume il est temps que tu viennes
> Pour que je sache enfin celui-là que je suis
> Moi qui connais les autres

[One day
One day I was waiting for myself
And I said to myself Guillaume it's time for you to come
So that I can know at last just who I am
I who know all the others][7]

The *eau de vie* motif is repeated in the etching that accompanies Apollinaire's 'Poème lu au mariage d'André Salmon' (Poem read at the wedding of André Salmon).[8] On the whole, Marcoussis accentuated the melancholy, nostalgic tones that are diffuse throughout the poems of *Alcools*.[9]

One of the more successful examples of collaboration as such, and one that reverses the usual process of text to image, is the series of woodcuts by Léopold Survage decorated with verses by Léonard Pieux (a pseudonym for the Baroness d'Oettingen) (see, e.g., plate 11).

On the whole the instances of collaboration would seem sufficient to put an end to discussion of the legitimacy of 'cubism' as a literary term. But collaboration is not identification. Does the cubist poem in itself exist? It must, since we find a definition of it, not in Paris, it is true, but in New York, in the *Poetry Handbook* of the American poet Babette Deutsch:

cubist poetry Heterogeneous images and statements, presented in a seemingly disordered but considered fashion, so that together they build a coherent work. It answers to Picasso's description of a paint-

Plate 2. *La Montre,* by Juan Gris (detail). Private collection. Courtesy of Esther Grether, Doetsch Grether & Cie Ag., Basel.

7. *Alcools,* in *Oeuvres poétiques de Guillaume Apollinaire,* Bibliothèque de la Pléïade (Paris: Gallimard, 1959), 74.

8. Ibid., 83.

9. See Anne Hyde Greet, *Apollinaire et le livre de peintre—Bestiaire,* Lettres Modernes (Paris: Minard, 1977), which also contains a fine analysis of Apollinaire's *Bestiaire* as illustrated by the non-cubist Raoul Dufy.

ing as 'a sum of destructions,' with the emphasis upon 'sum.' Like a cubist canvas, such poetry breaks down the elements of an experience in order to create a new synthesis and so represent it more truly.[10]

10. *Poetry Handbook: A Dictionary of Terms* (New York: Funk and Wagnalls, 1962), 42.

One cannot really argue with this succinct definition, but a listing of elements and devices common to the poetry and the painting helps to round out the picture. Picasso's 'sum of destructions' is a bit too broad. It could apply to omelets. Let us look for more precise attributes. There are, for instance, the notion of multiple perspective, which has a parallel in the shifting of personal pronouns (*je, tu, vous,* in 'Zone'); the concept of solid space, which finds an equivalent in the meaningful blanks between lines of verse; the recognition of the flat surface of the canvas, which has its analogue in the widespread use of the present tense; the view of art as experimentation, as suggested by Max Jacob's title *Le Laboratoire central*, and the contradictory view of the autonomy of the art object, held by Reverdy, among others; the attitude of willful negligence shared by Picasso, as a reaction to the 'finished' quality of academic art, and Apollinaire ('a pretty street whose name I've forgotten' ['Zone']); compare Cocteau's remark that modern poetry has taken off her evening gown and put on a negligee. Finally, there is 'simultanism,' one of those terms that changes meaning depending on whether it is used by painters (in reference to the contrasting colors of Robert and Sonia Delaunay) or by poets more or less synonymous with discontinuity or the juxtaposition of disparate phrases. The word became quite controversial just before the First

World War. It is a pity that no one in Paris bothered to quote Coleridge, who wrote, long before cubism, that the true poet is able to reduce 'succession to an instant.' Simultaneity in this sense is the property of all great poetry.

There is a field in which we find not only equivalencies but an actual borrowing of properties, namely, the field of signs, or 'semes,' the most prevalent being the letters of the alphabet. The cubists knew their Rimbaud. Picasso is said to have had a copy of *Illuminations* in the studio of the Bateau-Lavoir. Delaunay painted a watercolor illustrating the famous sonnet 'Voyelles,' which begins with the following line:

A noir, E blanc, I rouge, U vert, O bleu : voyelles

[A black, E white, I red, U green, O blue: vowels]

(see plate 3).

What intrigued the cubists was not so much the principle of synaesthesia, which had intrigued the Symbolists, but rather the shifting of the letters and words from their function as signifiers and their use as components in a cubist structure—the letter *J*, let us say, harmonizing with the curve of a bottle—or as more or less independent forms—the bulbous fragments of a letter *B* in a Léger painting, the Eiffel Tower-shape of an *A* in a Delaunay, the verticality of the four letters of the composer's name in Braque's *Homage to Bach*. Whatever meanings the words took on as combinations of letters, their shapes and colors conveyed the same aura of enchantment that Max Jacob described in his 'Petit Poème.'

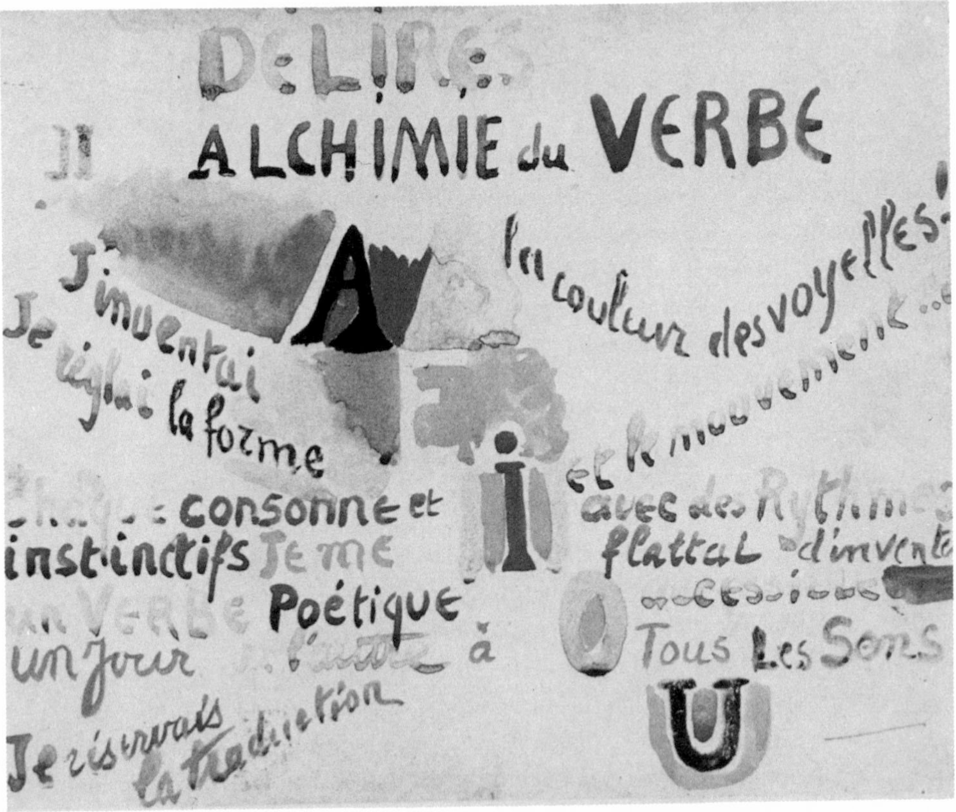
DELIRES
II
ALCHIMIE du VERBE
A
J'inventai
la couleur des voyelles!
la forme
et le mouvement
I
consonne et
instinctifs
avec des Rythmes
Je me
flattai d'inventer
Poétique
O
un Jour
à
Tous Les Sons
U
Je réservais
la traduction

But did the poets not have the right to protest this poaching on their preserves? Juan Gris, as we have seen, went so far as to insert an entire poem in one of his early cubist works. Serge Férat placed two open books with partially hidden lines of verse in the middle of his still life entitled *Le Livre* (ca. 1914), a title repeated in other works around the same time and indicative of the painters' enjoyment of their own bookishness.

The poets could not really complain, however, because they were doing much the same thing in reverse. 'I too am a painter,' proclaimed Apollinaire. It was not merely a question of calligrams and other kinds of visual poetry and typographical innovations but the attraction of geometrical shapes in the verbal imagery: rectangles, spheres, triangles, oblongs, ovals, and especially horizontal and vertical lines, which generated such images as towers, bridges, cords, rails, cables, rays, horizon lines, and so on.

So the poets borrowed from the painters, and vice versa. This practice of mutual exchange lay at the heart of the cubist movement and is something we can appreciate only by giving the poets their due.

In July 1914 Apollinaire, as if he sensed the approach of a vaster, more devastating conflict, of which he himself would become a victim, attempted to pacify the warring factions of Montmartre and Montparnasse with these words of moderation: 'The names of the various schools have no importance other than to designate this or that group of painters and poets. But they all share a desire to transform our vision of the world and to arrive, at last, at an understanding of the universe.'[11]

Plate 3. *Les Voyelles de Rimbaud*, by Robert Delaunay. Copyright 1991, ARS, N.Y./ADAGP. Color original.

11. Guillaume Apollinaire, *Apollinaire on Art: Essays and Reviews, 1902–1918*, ed. L. C. Breunig, trans. Susan Suleiman, Documents of Twentieth-Century Art (New York: Viking, 1972), 414.

In the pages that follow I have tried to take Apollinaire's advice to heart by putting more stress on the works of the poets and painters who composed the so-called cubist movement than on their theories and manifestoes, in the hope that these works will help to 'transform our vision of the world.'

THE CUBIST POETS

IN PARIS

PIERRE ALBERT-BIROT

1.

IV

cielbleu

s
t
r
e
v
s
n
i
p
a
Maisonsblanches   s

Tu offres ton corps chantant au sable à la mer au soleil Ton
corps est sablemersoleilmaisonsblanchessapinsverts

cielbleu

Que fais-je?

Je suis au coin du feu.

Il neige.

IV

bluesky

n
e
e
r
g
s
e
n
i
Houseswhite   p

You offer your singing body to the sand the sea the sky Your
body is sandseasunhouseswhitepinesgreen

skyblue

What am I doing?
I am sitting by the fire.
It is snowing.

From
*Trente et un poèmes de
poche* (Thirty-one pocket
poems), in *Poésie (1916–
1924)* (Paris: Gallimard,
1967), 15.

XV

Quel est cet enfant blond qui court en riant après ses billes de
couleurs?   *mes billes*
C'est moi
Et quel est le poète qui écrit ce poème?
Cet enfant blond qui courait en riant après ses billes de couleurs

■

XVII

La ville est sans péché
La neige lui a donné l'absolution
                    Un homme qui glisse
                              Un cheval qui tombe
Mais non la ville est en chemise de nuit

XV

Who is that blond child laughing as he runs after his colored
marbles?   *my marbles*
It's me
And who is the poet writing this poem?
That blond child who laughed as he ran after his colored marbles

■

From
Trente et un poèmes de poche, in *Poésie (1916–1924)*, 26.

XVII

The City is free of sin
The snow has given it absolution
                        A man who slips
                                A horse that falls
Oh no, the city is in a nightgown

From
Trente et un poèmes de poche, in *Poésie (1916–1924)*, 28.

Chez Paul Guillaume

Le 13e jour de Novembre en cette année 1917me
Nous fûmes chez le négrophile Paul Guillaume
Faubourg Saint-Honoré 108 à 8 heures
A quelque temps de là
Apollinaire arriva
S'assit sur une chaise en cuir et parla
D'abord d'un nouvel art qu'un jour il implicita
Quelque chose comme le technaphéisme
Dirai-je pour parler simplement
Et qu'un Américain a pu réaliser
Puisqu'on a pu photographier
Entre mai et octobre
Le premier plâtre à toucher
Ensuite Apollinaire a touché
La poésie non les poètes
Et nouvel Homme-Feu
Il nous a révélé tous les secrets des Dieux
Qui le tutoient
Si bien que maintenant tous ceux qui l'ont ouï
N'ont plus le droit de dire
Que dit donc ce poème ah je n'ai rien compris
Et puis ce fut du Debussy
Par-ci

In the Paul Guillaume Gallery

The 13th day of November in that 1917th year
We went to the gallery of the negrophile Paul Guillaume
108 Faubourg Saint-Honoré at 8 P.M.
A bit later
Apollinaire arrived
Sat on a leather chair and spoke
First of a new art that he came across one day
Something like 'technapheism'
If I may speak simply
And that an American brought about
Since it allowed one to photograph
Between May and October
The first touchable plaster
Next Apollinaire touched upon
Poetry not the poets
And as a new Man of Fire
He revealed to us all the secrets of the Gods
Who *tu* and *toi* him
So much so that all those who heard him
No longer have the right to say
What does this poem mean I didn't understand a thing
And then it was about Debussy
Over here

From
La Lune ou le Livre de poèmes (The moon or the Book of poems) (1924), in *Poésie (1916–1924)*, 237–38.

Les poètes X Y et Z par là
Et le PROFOND AUJOURD'HUI
De Monsieur Blaise Cendrars
Ce qu'a pensé l'auteur d'Henriette Sauret
Je le dirai quand je le saurai
Et ce furent trois interludes mis en musique
Comique
Par Auric
Et chantés par Bertin
On a beaucoup aimé ces trois petits morceaux
Qui s'en vont bien jusqu'à la fin
Et puis et puis ce fut Satie Erik
Qui Parada et disparut
Et Lara qui avait paru
Reparut
Et rythma quand même
Ainsi qu'elle l'avait voulu
Dans un silence de bréviaire
IL PLEUT d'Apollinaire

Et nous laissâmes la lumière
Pour la nuit de la rue

The poets X Y and Z over there
And the PROFOND AUJOURD'HUI
Of Monsieur Blaise Cendrars
And what the author thought of Henriette Sauret
I'll tell when I find out
And there were three interludes set to music
Comical music
By Auric
And sung by Bertin
We really liked those three little pieces
Which go right along until the end
And then and then it was Satie Erik
Who Paraded and disappeared
And Lara who had appeared
Reappeared
Even so reciting
Just as she had wanted
In religious silence
The IL PLEUT of Apollinaire

And we left the light
for the night of the street

Balalaïka

Poème à deux voix

       la balala   ika
Ferme les yeux pour y voir plus clair
        balalaïka
Que vois-tu
                 la la   i   ka
Des lampes de couleur qui font la ronde
   balala   la balalaïka
vivent et meurent   ombrelumière
    la   la   bala
vert jaune bleu   rouge   noir
        bala
et des mains qui aiment
    laïka
et des seins qui pointent
       balalaïka   laïka
et des seins qui penchent
    laïka
et des ventres et des trains qui sifflent
    balala   balala
et des eaux qui roulent et des monts
          lalaïka
glacés et des   *la   la   laïka*
la balalaïka   la   balalaïka   balalaïka
ïka la   laïka   balala   balala   balalaïka

Balalaïka

Poem for Two Voices

From
La Lune ou le Livre de poèmes, in *Poésie (1916–1924)*, 326.

     la balala   ika
Close your eyes to see more clearly
     balalaïka
What do you see
               la   la   i   ka
Colored lamps turning round
  balala   la balalaïka
live and die   shadowlight
     la   la   bala
green yellow blue   red   black
        bala
and hands that love
  laïka
and breasts that point
     balalaïka laïka
and breasts that tilt
       laïka
and bellies and whistling trains
    balala   balala
and rolling waters and mountains
       lalaïka
icy and some la la   laïka
la balalaïka   la   balalaïka   balalaïka
ïka   la   laïka   balala   balala   balalaïka

———— POÊME-AFFICHE ————

DERNIÈRE NOUVEAUTÉ

LAM
SOUVENIRS
INÉS

EN BOBINES DE
5 o o MÈTRES

CORDES
INCASSABLES
POUR

LYRES
ET
LUTHS

———— POSTER-POEM ————

LATEST NOVELTY

From *La Lune ou le Livre de poèmes*, in *Poésie* (1916–1924), 440.

LAM ORIES
MEMORIES
MEM INATED

IN 500 METER
SPOOLS

UNBREAKABLE
STRINGS
FOR

LYRES
AND
LUTES

PLACARD-POEM

THIS WAY ———————————— ☞

☜ ———————————— THAT WAY

1 K. 500

PARADISE

Follow to the end

Then you will ask the angels

From *La Lune ou le Livre de poèmes*, in *Poésie* *(1916–1924)*, 407.

POÊME-PANCARTE.

LE SOLEIL
EST DANS L'ESCALIER

POUR TOUS RENSEIGNMENTS
S'ADDRESSER PLUS LOIN
CHEZ LE MARCHAND DE VIN

PLACARD-POEM.
_____

THE SUN
IS IN THE STAIRCASE

FOR INFORMATION
CONTACT THE WINE MERCHANT
DOWN THE ROAD

From *La Lune ou le Livre de poèmes*, in *Poésie (1916–1924)*, 406.

Pierre Albert-Birot

Pierre Albert-Birot was born in Angoulême, in southwestern France, in 1876. Moving to Paris at an early age, he tried his hand at sculpture and painting before turning to experimental poetry with the founding of *SIC* (1916). During the four years that *SIC* existed, which was fairly long for an avant-garde magazine, Albert-Birot published poems by most of the members of the cubist group. The main condition for a poem's publication was that it express the spirit 'of the day.' (Albert-Birot even created an ism, nunism, from the Greek *nun*, now.) After the Italian futurists and Apollinaire, he sought to extend the frontiers of poetry by inventing new forms. He created hyphenated genres in the manner of Apollinaire's *poème-promenade* and *poème-conversation*, such as the *poème-affiche* and the *poème-pancarte* above.

Albert-Birot also wrote 'chronicle' poems, 'Chronique des Marins Americains,' 'Chronique-Jazz,' and 'Vernissages,' among others. 'Chez Paul Guillaume' is a chronicle in free verse that recalls a soirée in the gallery that first specialized in 'primitive' sculpture (see above).[1] Albert-Birot's first published volume (1917) he entitled *Trente et un poèmes de poche* (Thirty-one pocket poems), meaning not only poems of small format, or 'pocket poems,' but also those that illustrated his definition:

1. For a more complete version of 'tactile art' see Apollinaire's *Anecdotiques*, in *Oeuvres complètes de Guillaume Apollinaire*, ed. Michel Décaudin, 4 vols. (Paris: Balland et Lecat, 1966), 3:509–11.

Les jardins sont des poèmes
Où l'on se promène les mains dans les poches.

[Gardens are poems
Where you stroll with your hands in your pockets.]

Albert-Birot tried a wide range of visual poetry: poems arranged in geometrical shapes, rebus poems, calligrams, various kinds of alphabet and typographical play. Poem IV of *Trente et un poèmes de poche*, above, illustrates the connections between verticals and horizontals. It appeared at about the same time as the crossword puzzles in America.

In other poems the vocal qualities are stressed. A number are written to be performed. The text of 'Balalaïka' serves as a score for two voices. In the series named 'Poèmes à crier et à danser' (Poems for screaming and dancing) the sound effects are created by the repetition of letters, syllables, and inarticulate sounds. Like Apollinaire and later the dadaists, Albert-Birot seems to be shouting, 'On veut de nouveaux sons de nouveaux sons de nouveaux sons' (We want new sounds . . .).[2]

The alternation of words printed in italics and words printed in roman letters, as in 'Balalaïka,' was already a favorite device in a number of the pocket poems. In poems 'XV' and 'XVII,' above, the syntactic independence of certain line fragments invites the reader to make an 'associative leap.'[3] In 'XVII,' for example, lines 3 and 4, in italics, introduce incongruities that prepare the negation of the final line.

Max Jacob criticized Albert-Birot for an indiscriminate love of novelty,

2. Guillaume Apollinaire, 'La Victoire,' from *Calligrammes*, in *Oeuvres poétiques de Guillaume Apollinaire*, Bibliothèque de la Pléïade (Paris: Gallimard, 1959), 310.

3. In Guillaume Apollinaire, *Selected Writings of Guillaume Apollinaire*, trans. with a critical introduction by Roger Shattuck (New York: New Directions, 1950), 33.

claiming that every novelty appealed to him. Nunism can of course degenerate into faddism, and no doubt the volume entitled *Poésie (1916–1924)*, published by Gallimard in 1967, the year of Albert-Birot's death, contains its fair share of ephemera. That the poetry Albert-Birot chose to write was above all experimental should in no way imply a lesser gift. In any case, he was confident of his own talent, if we may believe this bit of advice 'Aux jeunes poètes' (To the young poets):

> Copiez copiez
> Religieusement
> La Vérité que vous êtes
> Et vous ferez un poème
>
> A condition que vous soyez poète
>
> Copy copy
> Religiously
> The Truth that you are
> And you will make a poem
>
> On condition that you are a poet[4]

The tremendous diversity that marks the 460 pages of *Poésie* in itself suffices to keep it fresh, as it reflects the inventive enthusiasm of its author.

4. Pierre Albert-Birot, *Poésie (1916–1924)* (Paris: Gallimard, 1967), 275.

GUILLAUME APOLLINAIRE

2.

A Linda

	Adnil	
	Danil	
	Nadil	
	Nalid	Alnid
	Dilan	Aldin
	Lanid	Ildan
Linda	Landi	
Ilnda	Naldi	
Nilda	Dalni	
Indla		
Indal		
Lnida		
Lndia		
Lndai		
Lidna		
Lidan		

To Linda

To

Adnil

Danil

Nadil

Nalid   Alnid

Dilan   Aldin

Lanid   Ildan

Linda   Landi

Ilnda   Naldi

Nilda   Dalni

Indla

Indal

Lnida

Lndia

Lndai

Lidna

Lidan

From
Poèmes retrouvés, in
*Oeuvres poétiques de
Guillaume Apollinaire*,
Bibliothèque de la
Pléïade, 2d ed. (Paris:
Gallimard, 1965), 665.

Chantre

Et l'unique cordeau des trompettes marines

■

Le Voyageur

A Fernand Fleuret

Ouvrez-moi cette porte où je frappe en pleurant

La vie est variable aussi bien que l'Euripe

Tu regardais un banc de nuages descendre
Avec le paquebot orphelin vers les fièvres futures
Et de tous ces regrets de tous ces repentirs
       Te souviens-tu

Vagues poissons arqués fleurs surmarines
Une nuit c'était la mer
Et les fleuves s'y répandaient

Je m'en souviens je m'en souviens encore

Un soir je descendis dans une auberge triste
Auprès de Luxembourg
Dans le fond de la salle il s'envolait un Christ
Quelqu'un avait un furet

Cantor

And the single straight cord of the trumpets marine

■

From *Alcools*, in *Oeuvres poétiques de Guillaume Apollinaire*, 63.

The Voyager

To Fernand Fleuret

Open up this door where I knock weeping

Life is as changeable as the Euripos

From *Alcools*, in *Oeuvres poétiques de Guillaume Apollinaire*, 78–80.

You were watching a cloud bank descend
With the orphan steamboat towards future fevers
And all those regrets and all that repentance
      Do you remember

Waves arched fish surmarine flowers
One night it was the sea
And the rivers spread into it

I remember I still remember

One evening I stopped at a sad-looking inn
Near Luxembourg
At the back of the room a Christ was taking off
Someone had a ferret

Un autre un hérisson
L'on jouait aux cartes
Et toi tu m'avais oublié

Te souviens-tu du long orphelinat des gares
Nous traversâmes des villes qui tout le jour tournaient
Et vomissaient la nuit le soleil des journées

O matelots ô femmes sombres et vous mes compagnons
                Souvenez-vous-en

Deux matelots qui ne s'étaient jamais quittés
Deux matelots qui ne s'étaient jamais parlés
Le plus jeune en mourant tomba sur le côté

            O vous chers compagnons
Sonneries électriques des gares chant des moissonneuses
Traîneau d'un boucher régiment des rues sans nombre
Cavalerie des ponts nuits livides de l'alcool
Les villes que j'ai vues vivaient comme des folles

Te souviens-tu des banlieues et du troupeau plaintif des paysages

Les cyprès projetaient sous la lune leurs ombres
J'écoutais cette nuit au déclin de l'été
Un oiseau langoureux et toujours irrité
Et le bruit éternel d'un fleuve large et sombre

Another a hedgehog
People were playing cards
And you had forgotten me

Do you remember the long orphanage of the train stations
We crossed cities that turn-tabled all day
And vomited at night the sunshine of the day

Oh sailors oh gloomy women and you my friends
        Remember

Two sailors who had never separated
Two sailors who had never spoken to one another
The younger one dying fell on his side

        Oh you dear companions
Electric bells of the stations song of the reapers
Butcher's sleigh regiment of unnumbered streets
Cavalry of bridges nights livid with alcohol
The cities I've seen lived like mad women

Do you remember the suburbs and the plaintive flock of landscapes

The cypress trees projected their shadows under the moon
That night when as summer waned I listened
To a languorous bird forever wroth
And the eternal noise of a river wide and dark

Mais tandis que mourants roulaient vers l'estuaire
Tous les regards tous les regards de tous les yeux
Les bords étaient déserts herbus silencieux
Et la montagne à l'autre rive était très claire

Alors sans bruit sans qu'on pût voir rien de vivant
Contre le mont passèrent des ombres vivaces
De profil ou soudain tournant leurs vagues faces
Et tenant l'ombre de leurs lances en avant

Les ombres contre le mont perpendiculaire
Grandissaient ou parfois s'abaissaient brusquement
Et ces ombres barbues pleuraient humainement
En glissant pas à pas sur la montagne claire

Qui donc reconnais-tu sur ces vieilles photographies
Te souviens-tu du jour où une abeille tomba dans le feu
C'était tu t'en souviens à la fin de l'été

Deux matelots qui ne s'étaient jamais quittés
L'aîné portait au cou une chaîne de fer
Le plus jeune mettait ses cheveux blonds en tresse

Ouvrez-moi cette porte où je frappe en pleurant

La vie est variable aussi bien que l'Euripe

But while dying there rolled towards the estuary
All the looks all the looks of all the eyes
The banks were deserted grassy silent
And the mountain on the other shore was clear

Then silently without one's seeing anything alive
Against the mountain there passed living shadows
In profile or suddenly turning their vague faces
And holding the shadow of their lances before them

The shadows against the perpendicular mountain
Would enlarge or at times suddenly shrink
And these bearded shadows would weep humanly
As they slipped along step by step upon the clear mountain

So whom do you recognize in these old photographs
Do you remember the day a bee fell in the fire
It was don't you remember the end of summer

Two sailors who had never separated
The older one wore an iron chain on his neck
The younger one braided his blond hair

Open up this door where I knock weeping

Life is as changeable as the Euripos

Zone

A la fin tu es las de ce monde ancien

Bergère ô tour Eiffel le troupeau des ponts bêle ce matin

Tu en as assez de vivre dans l'antiquité grecque et romaine

Ici même les automobiles ont l'air d'être anciennes
La religion seule est restée toute neuve la religion
Est restée simple comme les hangars de Port-Aviation

Seul en Europe tu n'es pas antique ô Christianisme
L'Européen le plus moderne c'est vous Pape Pie X
Et toi que les fenêtres observent la honte te retient
D'entrer dans une église et de t'y confesser ce matin
Tu lis les prospectus les catalogues les affiches qui chantent tout haut
Voilà la poésie ce matin et pour la prose il y a les
          journaux
Il y a les livraisons à 25 centimes pleines d'aventures policières
Portraits des grands hommes et mille titres divers

J'ai vu ce matin une jolie rue dont j'ai oublié le nom
Neuve et propre du soleil elle était le clairon
Les directeurs les ouvriers et les belles sténo-dactylographes
Du lundi matin au samedi soir quatre fois par jour y passent
Le matin par trois fois la sirène y gémit

Zone

In the long run you're tired of this ancient world

Shepherdess oh Eiffel Tower the flock of bridges bleats this morning

You've had enough of living in Graeco-Roman antiquity

Why even the automobiles look antiquated
Religion alone has stayed new religion
Has stayed simple like the hangers of Port-Aviation

You alone in Europe are not ancient oh Christianity
The most modern European is you Pope Pius X
And you whom the windows observe shame keeps you
From entering a church and confessing this morning
You read the prospectuses the catalogues the billboards that sing aloud
That's the poetry this morning and for the prose there are the
    newspapers
There are the 25 centime serials full of murder mysteries
Portraits of great men and a thousand different headlines

This morning I saw an attractive street—I've forgotten its name
All new and clean it was the sun's bugle
The directors the workers the pretty stenographers
Go up and down from Monday to Saturday four times a day
Three times a morning the siren groans

From *Alcools*, in *Oeuvres poétiques de Guillaume Apollinaire*, 39–44.

Une cloche rageuse y aboie vers midi
Les inscriptions des enseignes et des murailles
Les plaques les avis à la façon des perroquets criaillent
J'aime la grâce de cette rue industrielle
Située à Paris entre la rue Aumont-Thiéville et l'avenue des
    Ternes

Voilà la jeune rue et tu n'es encore qu'un petit enfant
Ta mère ne t'habille que de bleu et de blanc
Tu es très pieux et avec le plus ancien de tes camarades René Dalize
Vous n'aimez rien tant que les pompes de l'Église
Il est neuf heures le gaz est baissé tout bleu vous sortez du dortoir en
    cachette
Vous priez toute la nuit dans la chapelle du collège
Tandis qu'éternelle et adorable profondeur améthyste
Tourne à jamais la flamboyante gloire du Christ
C'est le beau lys que tous nous cultivons
C'est la torche aux cheveux roux que n'éteint pas le vent
C'est le fils pâle et vermeil de la douloureuse mère
C'est l'arbre toujours touffu de toutes les prières
C'est la double potence de l'honneur et de l'éternité
C'est l'étoile à six branches
C'est Dieu qui meurt le vendredi et ressuscite le dimanche
C'est le Christ qui monte au ciel mieux que les aviateurs
Il détient le record du monde pour la hauteur

A fretful bell starts barking around noon
The words on the street signs and the walls
The metal plates the notices screech like parrots
I love the grace of this industrial street
Located in Paris between the Rue Aumont-Thiéville and the Avenue des
    Ternes

That's the young street and you are still just a child
Your mother dresses you in blue and white only
You are very pious and with the oldest of your comrades René Dalize
You love nothing so much as the rituals of the Church
It is nine o'clock the gas light is turned down all blue you come out
    secretly from the dormitory
You pray all night in the school chapel
While eternal and adorable amethyst-colored depth
The flaming glory of Christ turns forever
It's the beautiful lily that we all cultivate
It's the red-haired torch that the wind never blows out
It's the pale vermillion son of the grief-stricken mother
It's the ever bushy tree of all the prayers
It's the double gallows of honor and eternity
It's the six-pointed star
It's God who dies on Friday and resuscitates on Sunday
It's Christ who goes up to the sky better than the aviators
He holds the world's record for altitude

Pupille Christ de l'oeil

Vingtième pupille des siècles il sait y faire

Et changé en oiseau ce siècle comme Jésus monte dans l'air

Les diables dans les abîmes lèvent la tête pour le regarder

Ils disent qu'il imite Simon Mage en Judée

Ils crient s'il sait voler qu'on l'appelle voleur

Les anges voltigent autour du joli voltigeur

Icare Énoch Élie Apollonius de Thyane

Flottent autour du premier aéroplane

Ils s'écartent parfois pour laisser passer ceux que transporte la Sainte-
    Eucharistie

Ces prêtres qui montent éternellement en élevant l'hostie

L'avion se pose enfin sans refermer les ailes

Le ciel s'emplit alors de millions d'hirondelles

A tire-d'aile viennent les corbeaux les faucons les hiboux

D'Afrique arrivent les ibis les flamants les marabouts

L'oiseau Roc célébré par les conteurs et les poètes

Plane tenant dans les serres le crâne d'Adam la première tête

L'aigle fond de l'horizon en poussant un grand cri

Et d'Amérique vient le petit colibri

De Chine sont venus les pihis longs et souples

Qui n'ont qu'une seule aile et qui volent par couples

Puis voici la colombe esprit immaculé

Qu'escortent l'oiseau-lyre et le paon ocellé

Pupil Christ of the eye
Twentieth pupil of the centuries he knows his business
And changed into a bird this century like Jesus rises in the air
The devils in the abyss raise their heads to watch it
They say it imitates Simon Magnus in Judea
They shout if it can fly call it a flier
The angels flutter around the youthful flutterer
Icarus Enoch Apollonius of Tyana
Hover around the first aeroplane
They make room from time to time for those transported by the Holy
    Eucharist
Those priests who are eternally rising as they elevate the Host
The plane finally lands without closing its wings
And the sky is filled with millions of swallows
Swiftly come the crows the falcons the owls
From Africa come the ibis the flamingoes the marabouts
The Roc bird celebrated by poets and tellers of tales
Soars holding in his talons the skull of Adam the first head
The eagle bears down from the horizon with its piercing cry
And from America comes the little hummingbird
From China have come the pihis long and supple
Who have but one wing and fly in couples
Then here comes the dove the immaculate spirit
Escorted by the lyre-bird and the ocellated peacock

Le phénix ce bûcher qui soi-même s'engendre
Un instant voile tout de son ardente cendre
Les sirènes laissant les périlleux détroits
Arrivent en chantant bellement toutes trois
Et tous aigle phénix et pihis de la Chine
Fraternisent avec la volante machine

Maintenant tu marches dans Paris tout seul parmi la foule
Des troupeaux d'autobus mugissants près de toi roulent
L'angoisse de l'amour te serre le gosier
Comme si tu ne devais jamais plus être aimé
Si tu vivais dans l'ancien temps tu entrerais dans un monastère
Vous avez honte quand vous vous surprenez à dire une prière
Tu te moques de toi et comme le feu de l'Enfer ton rire pétille
Les étincelles de ton rire dorent le fond de ta vie
C'est un tableau pendu dans un sombre musée
Et quelquefois tu vas le regarder de près

Aujourd'hui tu marches dans Paris les femmes sont ensanglantées
C'était et je voudrais ne pas m'en souvenir c'était au déclin de la beauté

Entourée de flammes ferventes Notre-Dame m'a regardé à Chartres
Le sang de votre Sacré-Coeur m'a inondé à Montmartre
Je suis malade d'ouïr les paroles bienheureuses
L'amour dont je souffre est une maladie honteuse

The phoenix that funeral pyre that engenders itself
For a moment veils all with its flaming ash
The sirens leaving their perilous straits
Arrive all three with their beautiful song
And all of them eagle phoenix and pihis from China
Fraternize with the flying machine

Now you are walking in Paris all alone in the crowd
As herds of bellowing buses drive by
Love's anguish tightens your throat
As if you were never to be loved again
If you lived in the old days you would enter a monastery
You are ashamed when you discover yourself reciting a prayer
You make fun of yourself and like the fire of Hell your laughter crackles
The sparks of your laugh gild the depths of your life
It's a painting hanging in a dark museum
And sometimes you go and look at it close up

Today you are walking in Paris the women are all steeped in blood
It was and I'd rather not remember it was at beauty's decline

Surrounded by fervent flames Our Lady looked at me at Chartres
The blood of your Sacred Heart flooded me in Montmartre
I am sick of hearing blessed words
The love that makes me suffer is a shameful sickness

Et l'image qui te possède te fait survivre dans l'insomnie et dans
    l'angoisse
C'est toujours près de toi cette image qui passe

Maintenant tu es au bord de la Méditerranée
Sous les citronniers qui sont en fleur toute l'année
Avec tes amis tu te promènes en barque
L'un est Nissard il y a un Mentonasque et deux Turbiasques
Nous regardons avec effroi les poulpes des profondeurs
Et parmi les algues nagent les poissons images du Sauveur

Tu es dans le jardin d'une auberge aux environs de Prague
Tu te sens tout heureux une rose est sur la table
Et tu observes au lieu d'écrire ton conte en prose
La cétoine qui dort dans le coeur de la rose

Épouvanté tu te vois dessiné dans les agates de Saint-Vit
Tu étais triste à mourir le jour où tu t'y vis
Tu ressembles au Lazare affolé par le jour
Les aiguilles de l'horloge du quartier juif vont à rebours
Et tu recules aussi dans ta vie lentement
En montant au Hradchin et le soir en écoutant
Dans les tavernes chanter des chansons tchèques

Te voici à Marseille au milieu des pastèques

Te voici à Coblence à l'hôtel du Géant

And the image that possesses you makes you go on living in
     sleeplessness and anguish
It's always near you this image that passes by

Now you are on the shore of the Mediterranean
Under the lemon trees that are in blossom all year long
With your friends you go for a boat ride
One is from Nice one from Menton and two from La Turbie
With horror we look at the octopuses down deep
And among the algae swim the fish that are images of the Savior

You are in the garden of an inn outside of Prague
You feel so happy a rose is on the table
And instead of writing your short story you observe
The rose beetle asleep in the heart of the rose

You are appalled to see your likeness in the agates of Saint-Vitus
You were deathly sad the day you saw yourself there
You resemble Lazarus crazed by the daylight
The hands of the clock in the Jewish quarter go backwards
And you too move slowly back in your life
Climbing to the Hradcany and listening in the evening
To the Czech songs in the taverns

Here you are in Marseilles among the watermelons

Here you are in Coblenz at the Hotel du Géant

Te voici à Rome assis sous un néflier du Japon

Te voici à Amsterdam avec une jeune fille que tu trouves belle et qui est
  laide
Elle doit se marier avec un étudiant de Leyde
On y loue des chambres en latin Cubicula locanda
Je m'en souviens j'y ai passé trois jours et autant à Gouda

Tu es à Paris chez le juge d'instruction
Comme un criminel on te met en état d'arrestation

Tu as fait de douloureux et de joyeux voyages
Avant de t'apercevoir du mensonge et de l'âge
Tu as souffert de l'amour à vingt et à trente ans
J'ai vécu comme un fou et j'ai perdu mon temps
Tu n'oses plus regarder tes mains et à tous moments je voudrais
  sangloter
Sur toi sur celle que j'aime sur tout ce qui t'a épouvanté
Tu regardes les yeux pleins de larmes ces pauvres émigrants
Ils croient en Dieu ils prient les femmes allaitent des enfants
Ils emplissent de leur odeur le hall de la gare Saint-Lazare
Ils ont foi dans leur étoile comme les rois-mages
Ils espèrent gagner de l'argent dans l'Argentine
Et revenir dans leur pays après avoir fait fortune
Une famille transporte un édredon rouge comme vous transportez votre
  coeur

Here you are in Rome under a Japanese medlar tree

Here you are in Amsterdam with a girl you find beautiful and who is
    ugly
She is supposed to marry a student from Leyden
Rooms are rented in Latin Cubicula locanda
I remember I spent three days there and as many at Gouda

You are in Paris before the examining magistrate
Like a criminal they put you under arrest

You went on painful and joyful trips
Before learning about lies and age
You suffered from love at twenty and thirty
I've lived like a fool and I've wasted my time
You no longer dare to look at your hands and every moment I'd like to
    sob
Over you over her whom I love over everything that horrified you
With your eyes full of tears you watch those poor emigrants
They believe in God they pray the women nurse their babies
They fill with their odor the waiting room of the Gare St. Lazare
Like the three Wise Men they have faith in their star
They hope to make money in the Argentine
And come back home with a fortune
One family carries a red eiderdown the way you carry your
    heart

Cet édredon et nos rêves sont aussi irréels
Quelques-uns de ces émigrants restent ici et se logent
Rue des Rosiers ou rue des Écouffes dans des bouges
Je les ai vus souvent le soir ils prennent l'air dans la rue
Et se déplacent rarement comme les pièces aux échecs
Il y a surtout des Juifs leurs femmes portent perruque
Elles restent assises exsangues au fond des boutiques

Tu es debout devant le zinc d'un bar crapuleux
Tu prends un café à deux sous parmi les malheureux

Tu es la nuit dans un grand restaurant

Ces femmes ne sont pas méchantes elles ont des soucis cependant
Toutes même la plus laide a fait souffrir son amant

Elle est la fille d'un sergent de ville de Jersey

Ses mains que je n'avais pas vues sont dures et gercées

J'ai une pitié immense pour les coutures de son ventre

J'humilie maintenant à une pauvre fille au rire horrible ma bouche

Tu es seul le matin va venir
Les laitiers font tinter leurs bidons dans les rues

La nuit s'éloigne ainsi qu'une belle Métive
C'est Ferdine la fausse ou Léa l'attentive

The eiderdown and our dreams are both unreal
Some of these emigrants stay here and lodge
In the Rue des Rosiers or the Rue des Ecouffes in little hovels
I've often seen them in the evening cooling off in the street
Like chessmen they rarely move
They are mainly Jews their wives wear wigs
They stay seated and anaemic at the back of the shops

You are standing at the counter of a low-down bar
You drink a two-sous cup of coffee among the outcasts

At night you are in a big restaurant

These women are not mean yet they have their problems
All of them even the ugliest have made their lovers suffer

She is the daughter of a Jersey policeman

Her hands which I had not noticed are hard and chapped

I feel great pity for the scars on her belly

Now I humble my mouth to a girl with a horrible laugh

You are alone the morning approaches
The milkmen clink their cans in the street

The night moves on like a beautiful mulatto
It's Ferdine the false or attentive Lea

Et tu bois cet alcool brûlant comme ta vie
Ta vie que tu bois comme une eau-de-vie

Tu marches vers Auteuil tu veux aller chez toi à pied
Dormir parmi tes fétiches d'Océanie et de Guinée
Ils sont des Christ d'une autre forme et d'une autre croyance
Ce sont les Christ inférieurs des obscures espérances

Adieu Adieu

Soleil cou coupé

■

Liens

Cordes *faites de cris*

Sons de cloches à travers l'Europe
Siècles pendus

Rails qui ligotez les nations
Nous ne sommes que deux ou trois hommes
Libres de tous liens
Donnons-nous la main

Violente pluie qui peigne les fumées
Cordes

And you drink this liquor burning like your life
Your life that you drink like an eau-de-vie

You walk towards Auteuil you want to go home on foot
To sleep among your fetishes from Oceania and Guinea
They are Christs of another form and another belief
They are inferior Christs of obscure hopes

Adieu Adieu

Sun clean-cut neck

■

Bonds

Cords *made of cries*

Sounds of bells across Europe
Centuries hanged

Rails that bind the nations
We are but two or three men
Free of all ties
Let's join hands

Violent rain that combs the smoke
Cords

From *Calligrammes*, in *Oeuvres poétiques de Guillaume Apollinaire*, 167.

Cordes tissées
Câbles sous-marins
Tours de Babel changées en ponts
Araignées-Pontifes
Tous les amoureux qu'un seul lien a liés

D'autres liens plus ténus
Blancs rayons de lumière
Cordes et Concorde

J'écris seulement pour vous exalter

O sens ô sens chéris
Ennemis du souvenir
Ennemis du désir

Ennemis du regret
Ennemis des larmes
Ennemis de tout ce que j'aime encore

Woven cords
Underwater cables
Towers of Babel changed into bridges
Spider-Pontiffs
All the lovers that a single tie has bound

Other more tenuous bonds
White rays of light
Cords and Concord

I write only to exalt you

Oh senses oh beloved senses
Enemies of memory
Enemies of desire

Enemies of regret
Enemies of tears
Enemies of all that I love still

Les Fenêtres

Du rouge au vert tout le jaune se meurt
Quand chantent les aras dans les forêts natales
Abatis de pihis
Il y a un poème à faire sur l'oiseau qui n'a qu'une aile
Nous l'enverrons en message téléphonique
Traumatisme géant
Il fait couler les yeux
Voilà une jolie jeune fille parmi les jeunes Turinaises
Le pauvre jeune homme se mouchait dans sa cravate blanche
Tu soulèveras le rideau
Et maintenant voilà que s'ouvre la fenêtre
Araignées quand les mains tissaient la lumière
Beauté pâleur insondables violets
Nous tenterons en vain de prendre du repos
On commencera à minuit
Quand on a le temps on a la liberté
Bigorneaux Lotte multiples Soleils et l'Oursin du couchant
Une vieille paire de chaussures jaunes devant la fenêtre
Tours
Les Tours ce sont les rues
Puits
Puits ce sont les places
Puits

Windows

From red to green all the yellow dies away
When the aras sing in their native forests
Pihi giblets
There is a poem to be written about the bird who has but one wing
We'll send it as a telephone message
Giant traumatism
It makes your eyes water
There's a pretty girl among the Turino maidens
The poor young man was blowing his nose in his white necktie
You will raise the curtain
And now there is the window opening
Spiders when the hands were weaving light
Beauty paleness unfathomable violets
We shall try in vain to have a rest
We'll begin at midnight
When one has time one has freedom
Periwinkles Catfish multiple Suns and the Sea Urchin setting in the west
An old pair of yellow shoes in front of the window
Towers
The towers are streets
Wells
Wells are public squares
Wells

From *Calligrammes*, in *Oeuvres poétiques de Guillaume Apollinaire*, 168–69.

Arbres creux qui abritent les Câpresses vagabondes

Les Chabins chantent des airs à mourir

Aux Chabines matronnes

Et l'oie oua-oua trompette au nord

Où les chasseurs de ratons

Raclent les pelleteries

Étincelant diamant

Vancouver

Où le train blanc de neige et de feux nocturnes fuit l'hiver

O Paris

Du rouge au vert tout le jaune se meurt

Paris Vancouver Hyères Maintenon New-York et les Antilles

La fenêtre s'ouvre comme une orange

Le beau fruit de la lumière

Hollow trees that shelter the wandering Capresses
The Chabins sing fatal melodies
To the cimarron Chabines
And the goose wa-wa honks in the north
Where the raccoon hunters
Scrape the fur skins
Sparkling diamond
Vancouver
Where the train white with snow and night fires flees the winter
Oh Paris
From red to green all the yellow dies away
Paris Vancouver Hyères Maintenon New York and the Antilles
The window opens like an orange
The beautiful fruit of light

Lundi rue Christine

La mère de la concierge et la concierge laisseront tout
    passer
Si tu es un homme tu m'accompagneras ce soir
Il suffirait qu'un type maintînt la porte cochère
Pendant que l'autre monterait

Trois becs de gaz allumés
La patronne est poitrinaire
Quand tu auras fini nous jouerons une partie de jacquet
Un chef d'orchestre qui a mal à la gorge
Quand tu viendras à Tunis je te ferai fumer du kief

Ça a l'air de rimer

Des piles de soucoupes des fleurs un calendrier
Pim pam pim
Je dois fiche près de 300 francs à ma probloque
Je préférerais me le couper parfaitement que de les lui donner.

Je partirai à 20 h. 27
Six glaces s'y dévisagent toujours
Je crois que nous allons nous embrouiller encore davantage
Cher monsieur
Vous êtes un mec à la mie de pain

Monday rue Christine

The mother of the concierge and the concierge will let everything
    through
If you are a man you will go with me this evening
All we need is for one of us to keep the outside door open
While the other goes up

Three gas jets lit
The boss's wife is consumptive
When you have finished we'll play a round of backgammon
An orchestra leader with a sore throat
When you get to Tunis I'll arrange for you to smoke some hash

That almost makes a rhyme

Piles of saucers flowers a calendar
Pim Pam Pim
Hell I owe my landlady almost 300 francs
I'd rather cut it clean off than pay

I'll be leaving at 8:27 P.M.
Six mirrors keep staring at each other
I believe we're going to get even more involved
Kind sir
You're a worthless guy

From *Calligrammes*, in *Oeuvres poétiques de Guillaume Apollinaire*, 180–82.

Cette dame a le nez comme un ver solitaire
Louise a oublié sa fourrure
Moi je n'ai pas de fourrure et je n'ai pas froid
Le Danois fume sa cigarette en consultant l'horaire
Le chat noir traverse la brasserie

Ces crêpes étaient exquises
La fontaine coule
Robe noire comme ses ongles
C'est complètement impossible
Voici monsieur
La bague en malachite
Le sol est semé de sciure
Alors c'est vrai
La serveuse rousse a été enlevée par un libraire

Un journaliste que je connais d'ailleurs très vaguement

Écoute Jacques c'est très sérieux ce que je vais te dire

Compagnie de navigation mixte

Il me dit monsieur voulez-vous voir ce que je peux faire d'eaux fortes et
    de tableaux
Je n'ai qu'une petite bonne

Après déjeuner café du Luxembourg

That lady has a nose like a tapeworm
Louise forgot her fur coat
I haven't got a fur coat and I'm not cold
The Dane smokes his cigarette as he consults the timetable
The black cat crosses the saloon

Those crepes were exquisite
The fountain is flowing
A dress as black as her fingernails
It's completely impossible
Here you are sir
The malachite ring
The floor is covered with sawdust
So it's true
The red-headed waitress was carried off by a book salesman

A journalist whom I know more or less

Listen Jacques what I've got to tell you is very serious

Shipping company passenger and freight

He said to me sir do you want to see what I can do with engravings and
    paintings
All I have is a little maid

After lunch Café du Luxembourg

Une fois là il me présente un gros bonhomme
Qui me dit
Ecoutez c'est charmant
A Smyrne à Naples en Tunisie
Mais nom de Dieu où est-ce
La dernière fois que j'ai été en Chine
C'est il y a huit ou neuf ans
L'honneur tient souvent à l'heure que marque la pendule
La quinte major

■

Fête

A André Rouveyre

Feu d'artifice en acier
Qu'il est charmant cet éclairage
    Artifice d'artificier
Mêler quelque grâce au courage

Deux fusants
Rose éclatement
Comme deux seins que l'on dégrafe
Tendent leurs bouts insolemment
IL SUT AIMER
       quelle épitaphe

Once there he introduces me to a big fellow
Who says to me
Listen it's charming
In Smyrna Naples and Tunisia
But where is it for God's sake
The last time I was in China
That makes eight or nine years
Honor often depends on the hour of the clock
The major fifth

■

Fete

To André Rouveyre

Fireworks in steel
How charming is all this lighting
    Artificer's artifice
Mixing grace with bravery

Two flares
Burst of pink
Like two breasts freed
Sticking out their nipples insolently
HE WAS A LOVER
        What an epitaph

From *Calligrammes*,
in *Oeuvres poétiques de
Guillaume Apollinaire*,
238.

Un poète dans la forêt
Regarde avec indifférence
    Son revolver au cran d'arrêt
Des roses mourir d'espérance

Il songe aux roses de Saadi
Et soudain sa tête se penche
Car une rose lui redit
La molle courbe d'une hanche

L'air est plein d'un terrible alcool
Filtré des étoiles mi-closes
Les obus caressent le mol
Parfum nocturne où tu reposes
    Mortification des roses

A poet in the forest
Watches indifferently
    His revolver on its safety-catch
Roses dying of hope

He dreams of the roses of Saadi
And suddenly his head bows down
For a rose reminds him again
Of a hip's soft curve

The air is full of a terrible alcohol
Filtered from the half-closed stars
The shells caress the soft
Nocturnal aroma where you are lying
       Mortification of roses

En Forme de Cheval

[Homme vous trouverez ici
une nouvelle représentation de l'univers
en ce qu'il a de plus poétique et de plus moderne
Homme homme homme homme homme homme
Laissez-vous aller à cet art où le sublime
n'exclut pas le charme
et l'éclat ne brouille pas la nuance
c'est l'heure ou jamais
d'être sensible à la poésie car elle domine
tout terriblement
Guillaume Apollinaire]

Horse

[Man you will find here
a new representation of the universe
at its most poetic and most modern
Man man man man man man
Give yourself up to this art where the sublime
does not exclude charm
and brilliancy does not blur the nuance
it is now or never the moment
to be sensitive to poetry for it dominates
all dreadfully
Guillaume Apollinaire]

From *Calligrammes*,
reproduced courtesy of
Rare Book and Manuscript
Library, Columbia
University, New York.

The original has a pink
wash of color over the
head, neck, and left
foreleg of the horse.

Jet d'Eau

[la lune ardente et toujours neuve
un bouton de rose doux comme un papillons (*sic*)
un jet d'eau
la queue d'un paon
un soir de neige
ciel constellé
un bombardement
un matin à New York
les lucioles
et tous les souvenirs
O quel bonheur que ce bleu ne soit pas mort encore
comme une fleur mourant entre
les mains d'un pâle soldat blessé]

Fountain

[the blazing moon always new
a rosebud gentle like a butterfly
a fountain
the tail of a peacock
a snowy evening
a star-spangled sky
a bombardment
a morning in New York
the fireflies
And all the memories
Oh what a blessing that that blue is not yet dead
like a dying flower between
the hands of a pale wounded soldier]

The original carries a delicate blue-gray wash suggestive of wind-caught spray.

Vase

[Pourquoi pleurer
Revenez demain
Il y a aussi des fleurs vénéneuses
et des fleurs toujours ouvertes le soir
elle aime le ciné
elle a été en Russie
L'amour marié avec le dédain
montre en perles
un voyage a Montrouge
Maisons-Lafitte
et tout finit dans les parfums
souvenez-vous-en
Laisse s'ouvrir la fleur et laisse pourrir le fruit
et laisse germer la graine
tandis que soufflent les tempêtes]

Vase

[Why weep
Come back tomorrow
There are also poisonous flowers
and flowers always open in the evening
she loves the cinema
she has been in Russia
Love married with disdain
Pearl-studded watch
a trip to Montrouge
Maisons-Lafitte
and everything finishes in perfumes
remember
Let the flower bloom and let the fruit rot
and let the grain sprout
while the storms rage]

From *Calligrammes*, reproduced courtesy of Rare Book and Manuscript Library, Columbia University.

In the original there is a rose wash over the vase, blue-black over the blooms, and a stroke of blue-gray over the stems.

Guillaume Apollinaire

Guillaume Apollinaire was the *nom de plume* adopted by Guillaume de Kostrowitsky, who was born in Rome in 1880 of an unwed Polish miss and an unknown father, probably an Italian army officer. He was brought up on the French Riviera by his baccarat-playing mother, and he spent a year as a tutor in the Rhineland before settling in Paris in 1902. With André Salmon he launched the avant-garde review *Le Festin d'Esope* (Aesop's banquet), which included Alfred Jarry among the contributors. His poems began to appear in the established Symbolist and neo-Symbolist periodicals. Apollinaire's first serious piece of art criticism, and the first to appear on Picasso, was published by *La Plume* in 1905. A three-way collaboration with the art dealer D. H. Kahnweiler and the painter André Derain produced the illustrated edition of *L'Enchanteur pourrissant* (The rotting magician) in 1908. That same year Apollinaire wrote the preface for the catalog of Georges Braque's show at Kahnweiler's, the first one-man show of cubist art. The first so-called cubist portrait, a portrait of Apollinaire by Jean Metzinger, was shown at the Salon des Indépendants of 1910.

By the year 1911, when he accepted the term 'cubism' on behalf of the painters, Apollinaire was ready to use every possible means to champion the new movement—the daily press (*L'Intransigeant, Paris-Journal*); the avant-garde magazines (*Montjoie, Der Sturm,* and especially *Les Soirées de Paris*); the Salons, where he helped arrange the cubist rooms (Room 41 at the Indépendants and Room VIII at the Salon d'Automne, 1911); public lectures such as the one on the different categories of cubism at the Section d'Or exhibit (1912); catalogue prefaces.

By the time the First World War broke out, in August 1914, Apollinaire had consolidated the position of cubism and gone on to support Italian futurism and to invent the term 'orphism' to designate what was to become abstract painting. Apollinaire's hope was to enroll all the new movements under a single banner that he called 'L'Esprit Nouveau' (New spirit). The term never quite caught on, perhaps because it was too general. Apollinaire himself, however, was the acknowledged leader of the avant-garde at the time of his death, in November 1918, when, already weakened by a war wound, he fell victim to the Spanish flu epidemic.

Apollinaire never applied the term 'cubism' to his own or others' poetry. Perhaps the closest he came was in a 1912 manifesto in which he spoke of 'painters and poets uniting to defend their plastic ideal.' Insofar as the devices of one medium find their equivalencies in those of another, it was inevitable that Apollinaire's poetry should contain cubist elements. Let us see how they appear in the texts presented above.

'A Linda,' an exercise written by Apollinaire at the age of twenty, is proof enough, if proof be needed, of his love of wordplay. He literally smothers a girlfriend, Linda Molina da Silva, with twenty-one anagrams based on her name. Could the name be more endearing than its bearer?

'Chantre,' published in *Alcools* (1913), is a one-line poem, a classical alexandrine based on a deceptively simple play of analogies: the similarity between *cor d'eau* and *trompette marine* (both literally meaning 'water horn') and the association between *cordeau*, a single straight cord, and the *tropette marine* as the name of a string instrument with only one string (see Molière's *Bourgeois gentilhomme*), a monochord that in turn evokes the solo voice of the cantor (*chantre*) of the title.

In *Les Peintres cubistes* (1913) Apollinaire relates an anecdote from Pliny.[1] One day Apelles landed on the island of Rhodes and called on Protogenes. The latter being absent, Apelles, instead of leaving his name, traced on a large painting in the studio a single line. On his return Protogenes recognized the hand of Apelles and traced on the line another of a different color, which gave the impression of three lines. Apelles returned the next day without finding Protogenes, and the fineness of the line he traced that day filled Protogenes with despair. And these almost invisible lines could not have been admired more if the painting had portrayed gods and goddesses.

Apollinaire thus attempts to strengthen his defense of 'pure,' or abstract, painting. But the anecdote would seem to be equally applicable to 'Chantre,' where the one line simultaneously contains five. And that one line, printed on the page, actually becomes what it describes.

'Le Voyageur' appeared in *Les Soirées de Paris* (September 1912) before its publication in *Alcools*. It turns the techniques of simultaneity inward upon the poet's deep solitude, which it relates to his sense of the in-

1. *Oeuvres complètes de Guillaume Apollinaire*, ed. Michel Décaudin, 4 vols. (Paris: Balland et Lecat, 1966), 4:286–287.

stability, the constant flux of existence. The two opening alexandrines, separated like two one-line poems, announce the dual theme. The first has all the dramatic urgency of an anguished cry emerging from nowhere. The second, which alludes to a strait in Greece famous for its surging currents and countercurrents, reads like an aphorism, a detached observation. The two together fuse the subjective and the objective views of the poet-traveler's condition. They also announce the form of the poem, which will consist of isolated and uncertain recollections and free associations surging forth helter-skelter from the memory of the poet, who may be addressing an unnamed interlocutor or, more probably, himself.

Fragments of remembered reality fall in alongside strange dreamlike scenes, such as the recurrent picture of the two sailors. There seems to be no rigorous necessity in the selection and arrangement of the 'old photos.' Apollinaire might have chosen others; these were simply the ones that tumbled out. The section that seems least automatic, consisting as it does of four highly polished alexandrine quatrains, is actually a kind of recollection in itself, an old manuscript of Apollinaire's that he has inserted as a private piece of collage. It is far from gratuitous, however. The silent, bearded shadows passing across a mountain, holding their lances before them, seem to emerge from the dim, mythical past of a Jungian memory. These lines cause the poem to open out into a mysterious new perspective in time.

The poem ends as it began. Nothing is resolved, but the two lines of the opening, enriched now by all the evocations within, restate with greater intensity the same sense of solitude and instability and even suggest as well the absurdity of this condition.

'Zone' appeared in *Les Soirées de Paris* (December 1912) before its publication as the liminary poem of *Alcools*. The action is much more precisely situated than in 'Le Voyageur.' Apollinaire called 'Zone' a 'poème-promenade'; and indeed the peripatetic motion governs the form throughout. The title suggests both the Parisian term for the suburbs surrounding the city and, etymologically, the beltlike or circular direction of the poet's walk, which continues from one morning to the next, interrupted by several stops (the Gare Saint-Lazare, a bar, a restaurant, a brothel) before the poet returns to his apartment in the suburb of Auteuil. The correlation between the ever-increasing fatigue of the walk and the despondency of the poet is implied all along.

Within this framework, which shows the real city unfolding before him, the poet introduces a series of memories from the various stages of his past life, and it soon becomes apparent that he is endeavoring to reconcile present and past time on a single plane, or more precisely, to reconcile his conflicting feelings towards two sets of opposites in time. The opening lines seek to proclaim enthusiastically the rejection of the past in its obvious connotation of 'old' in favor of the present as 'new.' But the ratio is not so simple. Line 25, 'Voilà la jeune rue et tu n'es encore qu'un petit enfant' (That's the young street and you are still a child), introduces a sudden switch, as in a chiasm. Newness becomes associated with the past, the poet's childhood, as he recalls his religious fervor at the

Collège Saint Charles; and the naive image of Jesus as an aviator, along with the imaginary parade of the birds that welcome the 'flying machine,' simply manifests a desperate effort to impose the enchantment of his boyhood faith upon the world of today. The attempt fails, and the sections beginning with the line 'Maintenant tu marches dans Paris tout seul parmi la foule' (Now you are walking in Paris all alone in the crowd) suggest the other pair of the reversed ratio. The present about him has lost all its freshness, and the poet finds himself overwhelmed by his despondency. As he continues his walk he desperately attempts once more to resuscitate his past in a series of rapid flashbacks, beginning with 'Maintenant tu es au bord de la Mediterranée' (Now you are on the shore of the Mediterranean), all moved into the present tense. Gradually, however, the magic of the memories pales, and nothing is left at the end but the pitiful sordidness of the actual city, with its emigrants and prostitutes. The poet makes his way home to sleep among the only remnants of his lost faith, the 'fétiches d'Océanie et du Guinée . . . les Christ inférieurs des obscures espérances' (fetishes from Oceania and Guinea . . . the inferior Christs of dark hopes). Daybreak, the hour for guillotinings in France, calls up through free association the final sinister image of the rising sun as a severed neck, 'Soleil cou coupé' (Sun clean-cut neck).

Its stark ending did not prevent 'Zone' from becoming the great avant-garde banner of modernism, and it is usually cited as the 'cubist' poem par excellence. No doubt it produces a fragmented, multidimensional effect through such devices as the telescoping of syntax, the almost exclusive use of the present tense, the rapid shifting of personal pronouns, the abrupt changes of locale, and the suppression of connectives and of course of punctuation. However, its basic structure remains sequential rather than simultaneous. If cubism is indeed a 'sum of destructions,' as Picasso claimed, in the sense that the fragmented elements of reality are rearranged so as to create a state of tension between the opposing forces of unity and multiplicity, then both the structure and the greater degree of polyvalence in 'Le Voyageur' make it more truly cubist than 'Zone,' which, for all its zigzags, flows along in time.

'Liens,' 'Les Fenêtres,' and 'Lundi rue Christine' date from the period 1913–14, when for Apollinaire experimentation replaces lyricism. They were published in the volume *Calligrammes* (1918) shortly before Apollinaire's death. In 'Liens' the diverse images all relate to the theme of bonds or ties announced by the title, and the poem's coherence derives from the harmonious fusion of the techniques of simultanism in the form and the ambivalent feelings towards interdependence that they express.

'Les Fenêtres' was written for the catalog of Robert Delaunay's 'Window' series. It is good example of a favorite French genre since the time of Théophile Gautier, the *transposition d'art*, brought to perfection no doubt by Baudelaire in 'Les Phares' (Limelights). In the *transposition d'art* the poet seeks to evoke with words the spirit or style of a painter or painting. 'Les Fenêtres' contains a variety of allusions to Delaunay and his work, but as Anne Greet points out, it is 'Apollinaire's own overwhelming reaction to a painter's work, and not that work as such, which dominates [the] poem.'[2]

2. Guillaume Apollinaire, *Calligrammes: Poems of Peace and War (1913–1916) / Guillaume Apollinaire*, trans. Anne Hyde Greet, intro. and commentary by Anne Hyde Greet and S. I. Lockerbee (Berkeley and Los Angeles: University of California Press, 1980), 350.

Apollinaire's reaction is expressed in a number of ways, including subtle wordplay, rhyme, and punning. The *vert* of the opening line, for example, connects at the end with the French pronunciation of Vancou*ver*, and then l'hi*ver*, again the *vert* of the opening line, and the final word lumi*ère*. In the third line from the end the listing of place names—a favorite device of simultaneity for Sonia and Robert Delaunay—includes for the French ear the homonyms, or approximate homonyms, *Hier* and *Maintenant* (yesterday, now). Time thus plays with space, and meanwhile the window opens out on the light, the light Apollinaire undoubtedly had in mind when he wrote in *Les Peintres cubistes*: 'J'aime l'art d'aujourd'hui parce que j'aime avant tout la lumière' (I love the art of today because above all I love light).[3]

'Lundi rue Christine' is a 'poème-conversation,' so named because it records the haphazard flow of real scraps and snippets of conversation around the poet as the pivotal point. Here Apollinaire pushes the cubist principle of fragmentation to the extreme. The blocks of words become shorter, the images and statements more heterogeneous. Notations replace complete sentences. Free, blank verse becomes the rule. Like the futurist *parole in libertà* (free words), the lines, if not always the actual words, have declared their independence.

August 1914 put an end to the experimental play of the prewar years. 'Fête' (*Calligrammes*) exemplifies the return to more traditional forms. It is one of a number of war poems that Apollinaire composed in the front-line trenches. The war sharpened his perception of the mysterious links

3. In *Oeuvres complètes de Guillaume Apollinaire*, 4:290.

between death and Eros. The privations of trench life and the constant presence of death acerbate the poet's desires to a point where he often fuses in richly ambiguous imagery the instruments of devastation and those of propagation, turning no man's land into a vast erogenous zone. Because of its restraint and concision, 'Fête' is perhaps the masterpiece of the genre. It consists of a subtly iridescent play between the triple analogy of bursting shell, rose, and bosom and the twofold sentiments uniting fear of death with erotic desire. The cubist elements have been toned down. Punctuation is absent as usual, and there is a bit of typographical play, especially in the second stanza, but for the most part the poem is made up of syntactically correct octosyllabic quatrains with regular rhyme.

Shaped poems, in which words are associated with design, were introduced by Apollinaire on the eve of the war. He called them *calligrammes*. The war prevented him from carrying out his original plan to publish them separately under the title *Et moi aussi je suis peintre* (And I too am a painter). He composed more during the war and made a selection of a score of them for inclusion among the eighty-odd pieces that make up the volume *Calligrammes* (1918). Among the most significant, no doubt, is 'Lettre-Océan,' the subject of a most perspicacious recent analysis by Roger Shattuck.[4]

The three calligrams above belong to a series that accompanies the catalog of a 1917 exhibit of the paintings of Léopold Survage and Irène Lagut.[5] I have chosen them for the graciousness of their design and for the mysterious fascination of their texts.

4. 'Apollinaire's Great Wheel,' in *The Innocent Eye* (New York: Farrar, Strauss, & Giroux, 1984), 240–62.

5. See Guillaume Apollinaire, *Oeuvres poétiques de Guillaume Apollinaire*, Bibliothèque de la Pléïade (Paris: Gallimard, 1959), 678–80.

The copies in color belong to one of seven sets that Apollinaire himself heightened, each one differently, with watercolors. The three calligrams reproduced here belong to set 6. The first is a eulogy of Survage in the shape of a prancing horse, apparently Pegasus, since it is the poetic qualities in the painting and indeed the poetry itself that dominate. The last line and the signature compose a kind of pedestal, balancing the weight of the horse and especially of the solidly placed hoof of the left leg, where the letters spell out the word *domine* (dominates). This verb leads in turn to a set of ambiguities, with which the poem concludes: Does poetry simply dominate (intransitive verb)? Does it dominate everything (*tout*) dreadfully? Does it dominate very (*tout* as adverb) dreadfully? Or is *tout terriblement* an epistolary formula like 'Yours sincerely' or 'En toute amitié': 'tout terriblement Guillaume Apollinaire'? In which case Apollinaire sees himself, much more than Léopold Survage, as a tragic poet in the year 1917. But can we be sure?

In the first of the two poems inspired by Irène Lagut the fountain, acting as an analogue to the style of the painter, becomes simultaneously a visual poem, with the jets of water rising and falling, and a verbal poem, with the disparate objects generated by free association coalescing to evoke the themes of death and dying in the last lines.

Despite the random nature of a number of the fragments that compose the third calligram—let us call it 'The Flower Pot' ['Vase']—and recall those of a 'poème-conversation' like 'Lundi rue Christine,' as a visual poem this work is quite closely connected with the flower motif of the written text. One might even imagine some of the lines of verse as the names of flowers in the manner of the *ne-m'oubliez-pas* (forget-me-not): 'Pourquoi pleurer,' 'Revenez demain,' 'souvenez-vous-en,' and so on.

Furthermore there is a clear distinction between the top part of the calligram, with its branches in bloom, and the pot itself, which contains within, both visually and verbally, the rotting fruit and the germinating seeds. Add to that the raging storms, and you have all the steps of a complete life cycle, with death and rebirth, as the poem concludes.

One ticklish question remains: Why on copy 6 did Apollinaire blot out with dark blue blossoms the lettering in 'The Flower Pot,' making it completely illegible?

3.

Prose du Transsibérien et de la Petite Jeanne de France

... Je suis en route

J'ai toujours été en route

Je suis en route avec la petite Jehanne de France

Le train fait un saut périlleux et retombe sur toutes ses roues

Le train retombe sur ses roues

Le train retombe toujours sur toutes ses roues

'Blaise, dis, sommes-nous bien loin de Montmartre?'

Nous sommes loin, Jeanne, tu roules depuis sept jours

Tu es loin de Montmartre, de la Butte qui t'a nourrie du Sacré-Coeur
    contre lequel tu t'es blottie

Paris a disparu et son enorme flambée

Il n'y a plus que les cendres continues

La pluie qui tombe

La tourbe qui se gonfle

La Sibérie qui tourne

Les lourdes nappes de neige qui remontent

Et le grelot de la folie qui grelotte comme un dernier désir dans l'air
    bleui

Le train palpite au coeur des horizons plombés

Et ton chagrin ricane ...

'Dis, Blaise, sommes-nous bien loin de Montmartre?'

Prose of the Trans-Siberian and Little Jean of France

... I'm on the way

I've always been on the way

I'm on the way with little Jehanne of France

The train makes a somersault and falls back on all its wheels

The train falls back on all its wheels

The train always falls back on all its wheels

From
Poésies complètes de Blaise Cendrars (Paris: Denoël, 1944), 70–72, 79–80.

'Blaise, tell me, are we very far from Montmartre?'

Far we are, Jeanne, you've been riding for seven days

You are far from Montmartre, from the Butte that nourished you, from
     the Sacré-Coeur you've huddled against

Paris has disappeared and its enormous blaze

Nothing's left but a stream of ashes

The rain that falls

The turf that swells

Siberia that turns

The heavy sheets of snow on the rise

And the tinkle-bell of madness that shivers like a last desire in the
     bluish air

The train throbs in the heart of the leaden horizons

And your sorrow sneers ...

'Tell me, Blaise, are we very far from Montmartre?'

Les inquiétudes
Oublie les inquiétudes
Toutes les gares lézardées obliques sur la route
Les fils télégraphiques auxquels elles pendent
Les poteaux grimaçants qui gesticulent et les étranglent
Le monde s'étire s'allonge et se retire comme un accordéon qu'une main
    sadique tourmente
Dans les déchirures du ciel, les locomotives en furie
S'enfuient
Et dans les trous,
Les roues vertigineuses les bouches les voix
Et les chiens du malheur qui aboient à nos trousses
Les démons sont déchaînés
Ferrailles
Tout est un faux accord
Le *broun-roun-roun* des roues
Chocs
Rebondissements
Nous sommes un orage sous le crâne d'un sourd . . .

'Dis, Blaise, sommes-nous bien loin de Montmartre?'

Mais oui, tu m'énerves, tu le sais bien, nous sommes bien loin
La folie surchauffée beugle dans la locomotive
La peste le choléra se lèvent comme des braises ardentes sur notre route

Worries
Forget your worries
All the stations full of cracks tilted along the way
The telegraph wires they hang from
The grimacing poles that gesticulate and strangle them
The world stretches lengthens and folds in like an accordion tormented
     by a sadistic hand
In the cracks of the sky the locomotives in anger
Flee
And in the holes,
The whirling wheels the mouths the voices
And the dogs of misfortune that bark at our heels
The demons are unleashed
Iron rails
Everything is off-key
The *broun-roun-roun* of the wheels
Shocks
Bounces
We are a storm under a deaf man's skull . . .

'Tell me, Blaise, are we very far from Montmartre?'

Hell yes, you're getting on my nerves you know very well we're far away
Overheated madness bellows in the locomotive
Plague, cholera rise up like burning embers on our way

Nous disparaissons dans la guerre en plein dans un tunnel
La faim, la putain, se cramponne aux nuages en débandade
Et fiente des batailles en tas puants de morts
Fais comme elle, fais ton metier . . .

'Dis, Blaise, sommes-nous bien loin de Montmartre?'

.   .   .   .

O Paris
Grand foyer chaleureux avec les tisons entrecroisés de tes rues et tes
    vieilles maisons qui se penchent au-dessus et se réchauffent
Comme des aïeules
Et voici des affiches, du rouge du vert multicolores comme mon passé
    bref du jaune
Jaune la fière couleur des romans de la France à l'etranger.
J'aime me frotter dans les grandes villes aux autobus en marche
Ceux de la ligne Saint-Germain-Montmartre m'emportent à l'assaut de
    la Butte
Les moteurs beuglent comme les taureaux d'or
Les vaches du crépuscule broutent le Sacré-Coeur
O Paris
Gare centrale débarcadère des volontés carrefour des inquiétudes
Seuls les marchands de couleur ont encore un peu de lumière sur leur
    porte
La Compagnie Internationale des Wagons-Lits et des Grands Express
    Européens m'a envoyé son prospectus

We disappear in the war sucked into a tunnel
Hunger, the whore, clings to the stampeding clouds
And drops battle dung in piles of stinking corpses
Do like her, do your job

'Tell me, Blaise, are we very far from Montmartre?'

.   .   .   .

Oh Paris
Great warm hearth with the criss-cross brands of your streets and your
       old over-hanging houses getting warm
Like grandmas
And here are the posters some red some green many-colored like my
       brief past of yellow
Yellow the proud color of French novels abroad
I love in the big cities to rub up against the passing buses
Those of the Saint-Germain-Montmartre line carry me up to assault the
       Butte
The motors roar like golden bulls
The cows of twilight graze on the Sacré-Coeur
Oh Paris
Central station for unloading resolutions crossroads of cares
The paint stores alone still have a bit of light on their
       doors
La Compagnie Internationale des Wagons-Lits et des Grands Express
       Européens has sent me its prospectus

C'est la plus belle église du monde
J'ai des amis qui m'entourent comme des garde-fous
Ils ont peur quand je pars que je ne revienne plus
Toutes les femmes que j'ai rencontrées se dressent aux horizons
Avec les gestes piteux et les regards tristes des sémaphores sous
    la pluie
Bella, Agnès, Catherine et la mère de mon fils en Italie
Et celle, la mère de mon amour en Amérique
Il y a des cris de sirène qui me déchirent l'âme
Là-bas en Mandchourie un ventre tressaille encore comme dans un
    accouchement
Je voudrais
Je voudrais n'avoir jamais fait mes voyages
Ce soir un grand amour me tourmente
Et malgré moi je pense à la petite Jehanne de France.
C'est par un soir de tristesse que j'ai écrit ce poème en son honneur

Jeanne
La petite prostituée
Je suis triste je suis triste
J'irai au 'Lapin agile' me ressouvenir de ma jeunesse perdue
Et boire des petits verres
Puis je rentrerai seul

Paris

Ville de la Tour unique du grand Gibet et de la Roue

It's the most beautiful church in the world
I have friends who surround me like guard rails
They are afraid when I leave that I won't come back
All the women I've met rise up on the horizons
With the piteous gestures and the sad looks of semaphore signals in the
    rain
Bella, Agnes, Catherine and the mother of my son in Italy
And the mother of my love in America
There are siren wails that tear my soul apart
Over in Manchuria a belly still quivers as though giving
    birth
I'd like
I'd like never to have made my trips
This evening a great love torments me
And in spite of myself I think of the little Jehanne of France
It was on an evening full of sadness that I wrote this poem in her honor

Jeanne
The little prostitute
I am sad I am sad
I'll go the 'Lapin Agile' to recall my lost youth
And drink some small glasses
Then I'll go home alone

Paris

City of the one and only Tower of the great Gibbet and of the Wheel

Denver, the Residence City and Commercial Center

DENVER is the capital of Colorado and the commercial metropolis of the Rocky Mountain Region. The city is in its fifty-fifth year and has a population of approximately 225,000 as indicated by the U. S. Census of 1910. Many people who have not visited Colorado, believe Denver is situated in the mountains. This city is located 12 miles east of the foothills of the Rocky Mountains, near the north central part of the state, at the junction of the Platte River and Cherry Creek. The land is rolling, giving the city perfect drainage. Altitude one mile above sea level. Area 60 square miles.

Ideal Climate, Superior Educational Advantages
Unequalled Park System

DENVER has the lowest death rate of the cities of the United States.

DENVER has 61 grade schools, 4 high schools, 1 manual training school, 1 trade and 1 technical school.

DENVER has 209 churches of every denomination.

DENVER has 29 parks; total area 1,238 acres.

DENVER has 11 playgrounds — 8 in parks, 3 in individual tracts.

DENVER has 56 miles of drives in its parks.

Commercial and Manufacturing City

Annual Bank C l e a r i n g s, $ 487,848,305.95.

Per capita clearings, $ 180.00.

Annual manufacturing output, $ 57,711,000 (1912).
Eighteen trunk lines entering Denver, tapping the richest agricultural sections of the United States.

DENVER has 810 factories, in which 16,251 wage earners were employed during 1911. The output of factories in DENVER in 1911 was valued at $ 52,000,000. The payroll for the year was $ 12,066,000 — OVER A MILLION DOLLARS A MONTH !

DENVER, COLORADO, BERLIN, GERMANY and MANCHESTER, ENGLAND, are cited by Economists as examples of inland cities which have become great because they are located at a sort of natural cross-roads.

For detailed information, apply to the *Denver Chamber of Commerce*.   *Prospectus free.*

From *Le Panama ou les Aventures de mes sept oncles* (Panama or the adventures of my seven uncles), in *Poésies complètes de Blaise Cendrars*, 94. Composed in English.

Contrastes

Les fenêtres de ma poésie sont grand'ouvertes sur les boulevards et dans
    ses vitrines
Brillent
Les pierreries de la lumière
Ecoute les violons des limousines et les xylophones des
    linotypes
Le pocheur se lave dans l'essuie-main du ciel
Tout est taches de couleur
Et les chapeaux des femmes qui passent sont des comètes dans
    l'incendie du soir

L'unité
Il n'y a plus d'unité
Toutes les horloges marquent maintenant 24 heures après avoir été
    retardées de dix minutes
Il n'y a plus de temps.
Il n'y a plus d'argent.
A la Chambre
On gâche les éléments merveilleux de la matière première

Chez le bistro
Les ouvriers en blouse bleue boivent du vin rouge
Tous les samedis poule au gibier

Contrasts

The windows of my poetry are wide open on the boulevards and in the
    shop windows

Shine

The precious stones of light

Listen to the violins of the limousines and the xylophones of the
    linotypes

The sketcher washes with the hand-towel of the sky

All is color spots

And the hats of the women passing by are comets in the conflagration of
    the evening

Unity

There's no more unity

All the clocks now read midnight after being set back ten
    minutes

There's no more time.

There's no more money.

In the Chamber

They are spoiling the marvelous elements of raw material

In the bistro

The blue-shirted workers are drinking red wine

Every Saturday a chicken for game

From *Dix-neuf poèmes élastiques* (Nineteen elastic poems), in *Poésies complètes de Blaise Cendrars*, 107–8.

On joue
On parie
De temps en temps un bandit passe en automobile
Ou un enfant joue avec l'Arc de Triomphe . . .
Je conseille à M. Cochon de loger ses protégés à la Tour Eiffel.

Aujourd'hui
Changement de propriétaire
Le Saint-Esprit se détaille chez les plus petits boutiquiers
Je lis avec ravissement les bandes de calicot
De coquelicot
Il n'y a que les pierres ponces de la Sorbonne qui ne sont jamais fleuries
L'enseigne de la Samaritaine laboure par contre la Seine
Et du côté de Saint-Séverin
J'entends
Les sonnettes acharnées des tramways

Il pleut les globes électriques
Montrouge Gare de l'Est Métro Nord-Sud bateaux-mouches monde
Tout est halo
Profondeur
Rue de Buci on crie 'L'Intransigeant' et 'Paris-Sports'
L'aérodrome du ciel est maintenant, embrasé, un tableau de Cimabue
Quand par devant
Les hommes sont

People are playing
They are betting
From time to time a bandit goes by in a car
Or a child plays with the Arc de Triomphe . . .
I advise Mr. Pig to lodge his protégés in the Eiffel Tower.

Today
Change of ownership
The Holy Ghost is being retailed in the tiniest boutiques
I read with delight the strips of calico
Of poppy
Only the pumice stones of the Sorbonne never bloom
The 'Samaritaine' sign ploughs through the Seine
And near Saint-Séverin
I hear
The stubborn clanging of the street cars

It's raining electric light-globes
Montrouge Gare de L'Est Métro Nord-Sud tourist boats world
All has become halos
Depth
On the Rue de Buci you hear *L'Intransigeant* and *Paris-Sports*
The airport of the sky is now, all in flames, a painting by Cimabue
When in the foreground
Men are

Longs
Noirs
Tristes
Et fument, cheminées d'usine

■

Ma Danse

Platon n'accorde pas droit de cité au poète
Juif errant
Don Juan métaphysique
Les amis, les proches
Tu n'as plus de coutumes et pas encore d'habitudes
Il faut échapper à la tyrannie des revues
Littérature
Vie pauvre
Orgueil déplacé
Masque
La femme, la danse que Nietzsche a voulu nous apprendre à danser
La femme
Mais l'ironie?

Va-et-vient continuel
Vagabondage spécial
Tous les hommes, tous les pays

Long
Black
Sad
And smoke, factory chimneys

■

My Dance

Plato excludes the poet from the city
Wandering Jew
Metaphysical Don Juan
The friends, the near-ones
You have no more customs and no habits yet
We've got to escape from the tyranny of the reviews
Literature
Poverty-stricken life
Misplaced pride
Mask
Woman, the dance that Nietzsche wanted us to learn to dance
Woman
But the irony?

Constant coming-and-going
Special kind of vagabondage
All men, all countries

From *Dix-neuf poèmes élastiques*, in *Poésies complètes de Blaise Cendrars*, 112.

C'est ainsi que tu n'es plus à charge
Tu ne te fais plus sentir . . .

Je suis un monsieur qui en des express fabuleux traverse les toujours
    mêmes Europes et regarde découragé par la portière
Le paysage ne m'intéresse plus
Mais la danse du paysage
La danse du paysage
Danse-paysage
Paritatitata
Je tout-tourne

■

Hamac

Onoto-visage
Cadran compliqué de la Gare Saint-Lazare
Apollinaire
Avance, retarde, s'arrête parfois.
Européen
Voyageur occidental
Pourquoi ne m'accompagnes-tu pas en Amérique?
J'ai pleuré au débarcadère
New York

That's how you're not a burden any more
You don't make yourself felt any more . . .

I am a man who in fabulous express trains crosses the ever-the-same
    Europes and looks glumly out the window
The landscape doesn't interest me any more
But the dance of the landscape
The dance of the landscape
Dance-landscape
Paritatitata
I all-turn

■

Hammock

Onoto-face
Complex clock-face of the Gare Saint-Lazare
Apollinaire
Speeds up, slows down, stops from time to time.
European
Western traveler
Why don't you go with me to America?
I wept at the dock
New York

From *Dix-neuf poèmes élastiques*, in *Poésies complètes de Blaise Cendrars*, 114.

Les vaisseaux secouent la vaisselle
Rome Prague Londres Nice Paris
Oxo-Liebig fait frise dans ta chambre
Les livres en estacade

Les tromblons tirent à noix de coco
'Julie ou j'ai perdu ma rose'

Futuriste

Tu as longtemps écrit à l'ombre d'un tableau
A l'Arabesque tu songeais
O toi le plus heureux de nous tous
Car Rousseau a fait ton portrait
Aux étoiles
Les oeillets du poète 'Sweet Williams'

Apollinaire
1900–1911
Durant 12 ans seul poète de France

The vessels shake the crockery
Rome Prague London Nice Paris
Oxo-Liebig makes a frieze in your room
The books stacked high

The blunderbusses fire coconuts
'Julie or I've lost my rose'

Futurist

For a long time you wrote in the shade of a painting
You dreamed of the Arabesque
You the happiest one of us all
For Rousseau painted your portrait
In the stars
The poet's pinks 'Sweet Williams'

Apollinaire
1900–1911
For 12 years the only poet in France

La Tête

La guillotine est le chef-d'oeuvre de l'art plastique
Son déclic
Crée le mouvement perpétuel
Tout le monde connaît l'oeuf de Christophe Colomb
Qui était un oeuf plat, un oeuf fixe, l'oeuf d'un inventeur
La sculpture d'Archipenko est le premier oeuf ovoïdal
Maintenu en équilibre intense
Comme une toupie immobile
Sur sa pointe animée
Vitesse
Il se dépouille
Des ondes multicolores
Des zones de couleur
Et tourne dans la profondeur
Nu.
Neuf.
Total.

The Head

The guillotine is the masterpiece of the plastic arts
Its click
Creates perpetual motion
Everyone knows the egg of Christopher Columbus
which was a flat egg, a fixed egg, the egg of an inventor
The sculpture of Archipenko is the first ovoid egg
Maintained in intense equilibrium
Like a motionless top
On its spinning point
Speed
It strips itself
Of its many-colored waves
Of its zones of color
And turns in depth
Naked.
New.
Total.

From *Dix-neuf poèmes élastiques*, in *Poésies complètes de Blaise Cendrars*, 126.

Académie Médrano

A Conrad Moricand

Danse avec ta langue, Poète, fais un entrechat
Un tour de piste
                sur un tout petit basset
                            noir ou haquenée
Mesure les beaux vers mesurés et fixe les formes fixes
Que sont **LES BELLES LETTRES** apprises
Regarde:
                      Les Affiches se fichent de toi te
                                mordent, avec leur dents
                                en couleur entre les doigts
                                de pied
La fille du directeur a des lumières électriques
Les jongleurs sont aussi les trapézistes
                      xuellirép tuaS
            teuof ed puoC
aç-emirpxE
Le clown est dans le tonneau malaxé
                    passe à la caisse
Il faut que ta langue   {   les soirs où
                    fasse l'orchestre
Les **Billets de faveur** sont supprimés.

Medrano Academy

To Conrad Moricand

Dance with your tongue, Poet, make an entrechat
Once around the arena

From *Sonnets dénaturés*
(Denatured sonnets), in
*Poésies complètes de
Blaise Cendrars*, 140.

              on a tiny basset-hound
                        black or hackney
Measure the measured verses and fix the fixed forms
That constitute the **BELLES LETTRES** mastered
Look:

                 The Billboards are bored with you
                      bite you with their
                      colored teeth between
                      the toes

The director's daughter has electric lights
The jugglers are also the trapeze artists
                   stluasremoS
        hsal pihW
taht sserpxE
The clown is in the mixing drum
              ⎰pay the cashier
Your tongue must ⎨   the evenings when
              ⎱play the orchestra
Complimentary tickets are out

Blaise Cendrars

Blaise Cendrars is the pseudonym of Frédéric Sauser, born in Switzerland in 1887. The new name, adopted during an early trip to Paris, suggests the notion of poetry as a process of combustion: *braise* (glowing ember), *cendre* (ash), *ardre* (to burn). Indeed there is hardly a photograph of Cendrars without the symbolic cigarette hanging from his lips.

Cendrars was an inveterate globetrotter, covering Europe, Russia, including Siberia, and both Americas. A sojourn in New York in 1911–12 inspired his first long poem, *Les Pâques à New York* (Easter in New York), written in loose, alexandrine couplets. It was with this manuscript in hand that Cendrars returned to Paris and soon befriended Apollinaire and the cubists. In fact Apollinaire's poem 'Zone,' also dated 1912 and also on the theme of loss of religious faith, bears such a striking resemblance to *Les Pâques* that a direct influence of the younger poet on the older is not ruled out.

Through Apollinaire Cendrars met the Delaunays and quickly assimilated their cubist doctrine of *simultanisme*. It was in collaboration with Sonia Delaunay-Terk that he wrote his next work, 'Prose du Transsibérien et de la petite Jeanne de France.' The text, comprising 446 lines of free verse (excerpts of which are shown above), was printed on a foldout album, which when completely open measures two meters in length. A color motif inspired by the text runs parallel to it for the entire length. Furthermore, if you multiply by two meters the 150 copies of the first edition (1913), you reach the top of the Eiffel Tower (300 meters).

This poem can certainly stand on its own merits, its coherence deriving mainly from the powerful impulsion of the Trans-Siberian train and the repetition of the refrain by the little prostitute Jeanne, 'Dis, Blaise, sommes-nous loin de Montmartre?' But it is the connections between the text and the color combinations of Sonia Delaunay-Terk, together with the format and its suggestion of the lengthiness of the Siberian rails, that concur to make of this work what the authors called the 'Premier Livre Simultané' (First book of simultaneity).

The next work, *Le Panama ou les Aventures de mes sept oncles* (Panama or the adventures of my seven uncles), also a travel poem, contains among other novelties a piece of literary collage, a facsimile of a prospectus issued by the Chamber of Commerce of Denver, Colorado (see above).

Cendrars then composed a series of short poems, also in free verse, under the title *Dix-neuf poèmes élastiques* (Nineteen elastic poems), a number of which first appeared in Apollinaire's cubist review *Les Soirées de Paris*. The title suggests that the reader is free to stretch each piece to whatever length he desires. Four texts are included above. In most of the texts, Cendrars proceeds by free association and discontinuity to create, with the help of the reader, a certain impulse, a degree of energy. 'Contrastes' is a phantasmagory of contrasting sights and sounds and colors of Paris, presumably inspired by the art of Robert Delaunay, with its 'simultaneous contrasts' and its series of 'windows' and 'Eiffel Towers.'

In 'Ma Danse' a sense of liberation is associated with the dance of the title, leading to a conclusion that is itself a dance.

It helps to know that 'Hamac' was originally entitled 'Apollinaire,' but some of the allusions remain obscure. Onoto was the name of a fountain pen, the advertisement for which apparently had a face resembling Apollinaire's. 'Oxo-Liebig' was a beef concentrate named for the inventor Justus Liebig. The other allusions would be known to most readers of the standard biographies of Apollinaire. The poem as a whole reads like a eulogy that is not free from barbs. The final lines, for instance, imply that in 1912 along came Blaise Cendrars.

In 'La Tête' Cendrars draws a formal analogy between various ovals—a decapitated head, an egg, a spinning top—in order to evoke the simultaneity of movement and immobility in the cubist sculpture of Archipenko, with its abstracted, oval-shaped heads.

Wounded during the war, Cendrars returned to civilian life in Paris and with the Swiss painter Emile Lejeune took over a studio in the rue d'Huyghens in Montparnasse, transforming it into a small concert hall and gallery (La Salle Huyghens) for poetry reading and musical sessions. It was here that Erik Satie and several of the composers who were later to be called Les Six congregated. By pure chance, one of the more notable poetry recitations also involved the number six. The program notes for

November 24, 1916, list the major cubist poets—Apollinaire, Cendrars, Cocteau, Jacob, Reverdy, and Salmon—reading their own poems along with 'the poems of a five-year-old girl' (apparently a niece of Cocteau). Cendrars read 'Contrastes.'

Cendrars also took part in what has been called 'the typographical revolution' of the century with his 'denatured sonnets,' such as 'Académie Médrano' (see above), with its reference to the Médrano Circus, on the slopes of Montmartre, regularly attended by Picasso's band.

At the end of the war Cendrars wrote an essay in which he claimed that cubism was the only ism strong enough to survive the war but that soon the word would have only a nominative value, designating a movement that lasted from 1907 to 1914. He named Picasso, Braque, and Léger as the three painters he most admired, and he wrote an essay on each of them in 1919. He collaborated with Léger on illustrated editions of *J'ai tué* (I have killed), a prose account of the horrors and absurdity of war,[1] and the apocalyptic *La Fin du monde* (The end of the world).[2]

Between the wars Cendrars resumed his travels, living mainly in South America and writing travelogues, essays, and novels. He lived through the German occupation in southern France and died in Paris in 1961.

1. *J'ai tué* (Paris: La Belle Edition, 1918), a limited edition of 176 copies, with five drawings by Fernand Léger.

2. *La Fin du monde*, cover illustration for Cendrars's *J'ai tué* (see Burr Wallen and Donna Stein, *The Cubist Print* [Santa Barbara: University Art Museum, University of California, 1981], 202).

JEAN COCTEAU

4.

Féerie

Après PARADE la petite fille américaine sortit du théâtre. C'était le théâtre du Châtelet où elle aurait dû voir Les Pilules du Diable, La Biche au bois, La poudre de Perlinpinpin, Le Tour du Monde. On l'avait huée. Elle portait sur la tête un papillon du Brésil et un col marin dans le dos. Le tout coûtait trente francs au bazar. Nous l'avions acheté avec le peintre et le danseur russe. Elle aussi était russe, ce qui est triste pour une petite fille américaine. Elle faisait des signes de croix, se tirait les cartes, fumait et pleurait beaucoup. Elle voulut tout de suite partir pour New-York où les petites filles ne sont pas russes et reçoivent des nouvelles de leur famille. Mais les bateaux et les maisons d'Amérique sont trop grands. On raconte même que les ascenseurs vous ouvrent le ventre et vous le recousent vide. Et puis elle avait peur des nègres qui s'approchent la nuit sans être vus.

PARADE jouet mécanique d'un modèle qui ne marche pas tout seul. Il fallait encore du courage.

Les arbres du printemps sont à l'envers et avant de sauter dans la bouche d'ogre en or et en obscurité qui siffle, elle me pince de toutes ses forces.

C'est moi qui fais le bruit des vagues.

Allons, Marie.

Fairy Scene

After *Parade* the little American girl left the theater. It was the Châtelet, From Jean Cocteau, *Poésie* (Paris: Gallimard, 1920). where she should have seen the Devil's Pills, the Hind in the Woods, the Powder of Perlimpinpin, Around the World. They had booed her. On her head she wore a butterfly from Brazil and a sailor's collar on her back. It had all cost thirty francs at the bazaar. We had bought it with the painter and the Russian dancer. She too was Russian, which is sad for a little American girl. She made the sign of the cross, told fortunes with playing cards, smoked and wept a lot. She wanted to leave right away for New York, where the little girls are not Russian and get news from the family. But the boats and the houses in America are too big. They even say that the elevators open up your stomach and sew it up again empty. And she was afraid of the Negroes, who come close at night without being seen.

Parade, a mechanical toy of a model that won't work by itself. You had to have more courage.

The springtime trees are on the wrong side, and before jumping into the mouth of the golden ogre and into the darkness that hisses she pinches me with all her might.

I'm the one who makes the noise of the waves.

Let's go, Marie.

Le Cap de Bonne-Espérance

. . . Préambule

Ebauche
d'un art poétique

.   .   .   .   .   .

Désengluons-nous de nos rêves

Le grain de seigle
sans babil d'herbe
et loin des arbres orateurs

je

le

plante

Il   germera

Mais renonce aux noces champêtres

Car le verbe explosif tombe sans faire de mal
éternel à travers
les générations compactes

The Cape of Good Hope

. . . Preamble

A rough draft
for an ars poetica

From *Le Cap de Bonne-Espérance* (The Cape of Good Hope) (Paris: Gallimard, 1919), 28, 35.

.   .   .   .

Let's get our dreams unstuck

The grain of rye
free from the prattle of grass
and far from the declaiming trees

I

plant

it

It   will sprout

But forget about the rustic festivities

For the explosive word falls harmlessly
eternal through
the compact generations

et sinon toi

      rien

      ne percute

sa dynamite embaumée

Salut
j'écarte l'éloquence
la voile creuse
et la voile grosse
qui font dévier le vaisseau

Mon encre encoche
et là

et là

            et là

et
là

dort
la profonde poésie

L'armoire à glace charriant des banquises
la petite esquimaude

and except for you

> nothing
> detonates

its sweet-scented dynamite

Greetings
I discard eloquence
the empty sail
and the swollen sail
which cause the ship to lose her course

My ink nicks
and there

and there

> and there

and
there

sleeps
deep poetry

The mirror-paneled wardrobe washing down ice-floes
the little eskimo girl

qui rêve
en boule
aux nègres moites
elle y avait le nez
        aplati
contre la vitre des Noëls tristes

Un ours blanc
chamarré de moires chromatiques

se sèche au soleil de minuit

Paquebots

L'énorme chose de luxe

lente à descendre
avec toutes ses lumières

ainsi
sombre le bal
dans les mille miroirs du palace

Et maintenant
c'est moi

dreaming
in a heap
of moist negroes
her nose was
        flattened
against the window-pane of dreary Christmases

A white bear
adorned with chromatic moire

dries himself in the midnight sun

Liners

The huge luxury item

Slowly founders
all its lights aglow

and so
sinks the evening-dress ball
into the thousand mirrors of the palace hotel

And now
it is I

maigre Colomb des phénomènes
seul
devant une armoire à glace
pleine de linge
et qui ferme à clef

Le mineur opiniâtre
du vide
exploite
sa mine féconde

le possibile brut
y   miroite
emmèlé à sa roche blanche

    O
    princesse du sommeil fou
écoute mon cor
       et ma meute

Je te délivre
de la forêt
où nous surprimâmes l'enchantement

the thin Columbus of phenomena
alone
in front of a mirror-paneled wardrobe
full of linen
and locking with a key

The obstinate miner
of the void
exploits
his fertile mine

the potential in the rough
glitters   there
mingling with its white rock

   Oh
      princess of the mad sleep
listen to my horn
            and my pack of hounds

I deliver you
from the forest
where we came upon the spell

Nous voici
par la plume
l'un à l'autre
mariés
sur la page

Iles   sanglots d'Ariane

les Ariane
            se   trainant
        les Ariane   les otaries

car je vous trompe mes belles strophes
pour
courir éveiller
ailleurs

Je ne prémédite aucune architecture

Simplement
sourd
comme toi   Beethoven

aveugle

Here we are
by the pen
one with the other
wedded
on the page

Isles   sobs of Ariadne

Ariadnes
          dragging   along
          Ariadnes   seals

for I betray you my fair stanzas
to
run and awaken
elsewhere

I plan no architecture

Simply
deaf
like you   Beethoven

blind

comme toi
Homère
vieillard innombrable

né partout

j'élabore
dans les prairies du silence
intérieur

et l'oeuvre de la mission
et le poème de l'oeuvre
et la strophe du poème
et le groupe de la strophe
et les mots du groupe
et les lettres du mot
et   la moindre
boucle des lettres

c'est ton pied
de satin attentif
que je pose
danseur de corde
rose

like you
Homer
numberless old man

born everywhere

I elaborate
in the prairies of inner
silence

and the work of the mission
and the poem of the work
and the stanza of the poem
and the group of the stanza
and the words of the group
and the letters of the word
and   the least
loop of the letters

it's your foot
of attentive satin
that I place in position
pink
tightrope walker

aspiré par le vide

à gauche   à droite
le dieu secoue
et je marche
vers l'autre rive
                 avec une précaution infinie

sucked up by the void

to the left   to the right
the god gives a shake
and I walk
toward the other side
        with infinite precaution

Jean Cocteau

Born in 1889 in Maisons-Laffitte, a suburb of Paris, Jean Cocteau was brought up in the comfortable circumstances of the *haute bourgeoisie*. He might have been nothing more than a Parisian dilettante had he not come into contact with Serge Diaghilev's Ballets Russes in 1910. Cocteau, already an accomplished artist, was commissioned by Diaghilev to paint the posters for the premiere of *Spectre de la Rose* (1911). The *Sacre du Printemps* (Rites of spring) performance in 1913 with Nijinsky overwhelmed him, and from that moment he was determined to revolutionize the ballet as a genre.

In the theme of the parade Cocteau found a subject both popular and avant-garde. Having written the scenario for *Parade*, he persuaded Erik Satie and Picasso, whom he had just met, to do the score and the set. He overcame the hesitations of Massine as choreographer and the indifference of Diaghilev, who was no modernist, and succeeded, by prodding and cajoling each of these prima donnas, in creating the 'first cubist ballet.'

Parade was presented at the Théâtre du Châtelet on May 18, 1917. While not exactly the *succès de scandale* that Cocteau claimed it to be, *Parade*, along with Apollinaire's *Les Mamelles de Tirésias* (The bosoms of

Tiresias), presented in June, paved the way for modernism on the French stage.

The French word *parade* designates the performance, similar to that of a barker, in front of a circus sideshow. Will the public go inside? With Cocteau, we soon come to discover, the real performance is the one outside, on the street. The performers are a Chinaman, an American girl, two acrobats, as well as the 'managers' (the word is in English) created by Picasso as walking, cardboard skyscrapers.

In a later commentary on *Parade* Cocteau, who delighted in paradox, claimed that the four performers, rather than Picasso's monsters, justify the adjective 'cubist.' For the four performers cubism involved changing 'real gestures' into dance, just as a cubist painter transforms reality into 'pure painting' without losing sight of the real. And Cocteau gives examples of 'real gestures.' The little girl, for instance, races, cycles, imitates Charlie Chaplin, does a ragtime, gets shipwrecked, takes a Kodak picture, and so on.

At Cocteau's insistence Satie added sound effects to the score: the noise of a typewriter, a telegraph key, a siren, an airplane, and others. And here too he justifies such innovations by analogy with cubist painting; the noises, he claims, are examples of 'trompe-l'oreille,' comparable to the trompe-l'oeil of the painters (newspaper, cornice, imitation wood).

Cocteau commemorated the premiere of *Parade* with the prose poem 'Féerie' (see above). Less directly there emerged from the rehearsals of the ballet, the changes in script, and the almost daily contact with Picasso a feeling of admiration, which the poet expressed in a poem entitled *L'Ode à Picasso*.[1] The relatively short text is so scattered—sometimes there are only two or three words to a page—that one inevitably links it to the typographical innovations of Mallarmé's *Un Coup de dés jamais n'abolira le hasard* (A throw of the dice will never abolish chance).

The *Ode* alludes to details of Picasso's life—Montparnasse 'Ma jolie,' Nadar—and goes on to underline his struggle with the Muses. He pays the price for having scoffed at them, for he is caught in their dreadful round and tries desperately to get out.

If for Cocteau, as for Pascal and Malraux, the prison cell is the metaphor for the human condition, Picasso would seem to be simultaneously prisoner and liberator. His painting *is* his liberation, his 'way of getting out.'

In 1918 Cocteau founded a publishing house with Blaise Cendrars, Les Editions de la Sirène, which put out Cendrars's *Panama* and Cocteau's next work, *Le Cap de Bonne-Espérance*, which he wrote in memory of the World War I ace Garros, 'mort pour la France' (died for France). Like the *Ode à Picasso*, it is a typographical experiment in which the seemingly helter-skelter placement of the words and phrases serves as a verbal imitation of the action. In a preliminary section Cocteau has set forth in the same style the draft of a cubist ars poetica. Stating that he 'plans no architecture,' he allows the images to fall where they will, each one rounding out the poet's notion of his art: the germinating grain, the explosive word, the sail as a symbol of rhetoric, the mirror as an entranceway, the

1. *Entre Picasso et Radiguet*, Collection Miroirs de l'art (Paris: Hermann, 1968), 129–92.

sinking of the *Titanic,* Columbus as explorer, the miner as prospector, the sleeping beauty, the acrobat, and still others that share the quality of 'le possible brut' (the potential in the rough). The printed pages thus are the stage for a series of typographical performances, such as the following:

Mon encre encoche

et là

　　　　et là

et
là

dort
la profonde poésie

Cocteau enjoyed reading from *Le Cap de Bonne-Espérance* at private gatherings.[2] He had a resonant voice and perfect diction. Listen to his masterful role as narrator in the Cocteau-Stravinsky oratorio *Oedipus Rex,* including the full strength he gives the aspirate *h* when Oedipus falls: 'Il tombe de *h*aut!' (He falls from *h*igh up).

Cocteau's cubist phase was rather short-lived but sufficiently important to justify the epithet, whose use Cocteau, unlike most of the other poets in the group, encouraged.

2. Francis Steegmuller describes one of these readings, including Cocteau's rage against Proust for arriving three hours late, in *Cocteau: A Biography* (Boston: Little, Brown, 1970), 233–34.

SONIA DELAUNAY

5.

[Zenith]

ZENITH / MIDI BAT / Sur son enclume solaire / les Rayons de la Lumière

■

[Salut, Blaise Cendrars]

Je vis, à un des mercredis d'Apollinaire, assis sur son grand divan, un petit jeune homme frêle et blond, qu'il nous présenta comme Blaise Cendrars.

On dut sympathiser, car le lendemain, Cendrars était chez nous et nous apportait une petite plaquette qui s'appelait : 'LES PAQUES' et était éditée par 'Les Hommes Nouveaux'.

Je lus ce poème la première et le passai à Delaunay, enthousiasmée par le souffle nouveau qui s'en dégageait.

Le poème fut relié par moi-même, précieusement, avec une peau de chamois sur laquelle je plaquai des motifs de papier collés. A l'intérieur, je fis de même, avec de grands carrés de papier de couleur. C'était ma réponse plastique à la beauté du poème à partir duquel, datait notre amitié avec Cendrars.

Il devint notre habitué de tous les jours et Apollinaire fut un peu jaloux de l'amitié et de l'admiration que nous eûmes pour Cendrars.

Tout cela se passait au Début de 1913 . . . deux mois plus tard Cendrars apporta son poème du 'TRANSSIBÉRIEN' et de 'LA PETITE JEHANNE DE

[Zenith]

ZENITH / NOON beats out / on its solar anvil / the rays of light

Poster-poem, frontispiece for the review *Risques*, special issue 9 / 10, *Salut Blaise Cendrars* (1950–54).

■

[Greetings, Blaise Cendrars]

At one of Apollinaire's Wednesdays I saw, sitting on the big divan, a tiny young man, frail and blond, whom Apollinaire introduced as Blaise Cendrars.

From *Risques*, special issue 9 / 10, *Salut Blaise Cendrars*, 23–24.

We must have got along because the next day Cendrars came to our home and brought us a little plaquette entitled *Les Pâques*, published by 'Les Hommes Nouveaux.'

I read the poem first, then handed it to Delaunay, delighted by its newness, its originality.

I bound the book preciously in chamois on which I laid several motifs of *papier collé*. I did the same on the inside with large squares of colored paper. This was my response to the beauty of the poem. And that was the beginning of our friendship with Cendrars.

He became a regular and Apollinaire was a little jealous of our friendship and admiration for Cendrars.

All that took place in early 1913. Two months later Cendrars brought us his poem of the 'Transsibérien' and 'La Petite Jehanne de France' *[sic]*.

FRANCE' et, comme il venait d'hériter d'une tante, il mit toute la somme reçue dans l'Edition de ce poème. Nous décidâmes de le faire dépliant sur deux mètres, un motif coloré accompagnant le texte. Je m'inspirai du texte pour une harmonie de couleurs qui se déroulait parallèlement au beau poème. Les lettres d'impression furent choisies par nous, de différents types et grandeurs, choses qui étaient révolutionnaires pour l'époque. Le fond du texte était coloré pour s'harmoniser avec l'illustration. Je composai un bulletin, exécuté aussi au pochoir, où fond et lettres s'harmonisaient en contrastes simultanés.

Le bulletin fut envoyé à la presse et nous reçûmes des critiques du monde entier, en toutes langues. . . .

En repensant à ces temps lointains, je crois que Cendrars était de ces poètes qui vivent leur poésie. Il nous a apporté le souffle du large, la curiosité des voyages lointains, cet air épicé des pays exotiques. . . .

And as he had just received an inheritance from an aunt he put the entire sum into the publishing of this poem. We decided to make it a fold-out two meters long with a color motif accompanying the text. I was inspired by the text to make a harmonious arrangement of colors that would unroll parallel to the poem. We chose printer's characters of different types and sizes — something that was quite revolutionary for that period. The background of the text was colored to go with my illustration. I composed a flyer which was also done in *pochoir* (stencil) where background and letters harmonized in simultaneous contrasts. We sent it off to the press and received reviews all over the world in every language. . . .

As I look back on those days I think that Cendrars was one of those poets who live their poetry. He brought us the breath of the wide-open spaces, the curiosity of distant voyages, that spicy air of exotic lands. . . .

Sonia Delaunay

Sonia Delaunay-Terk, born in the Ukraine in 1885, settled in Paris in 1906. Her early paintings show a marked influence of Gauguin and Van Gogh. After an unsuccessful marriage with Wilhelm Uhde, the art dealer, ended in divorce, she married Robert Delaunay in 1910. Their collaboration led them through cubism to an intensely colored abstract style that Apollinaire baptized 'orphism.'

It was still during the cubist phase that Sonia began experimenting with new poetic forms. Everything became a 'poem' for her. The Delaunay apartment was filled with 'curtain poems,' 'dress poems,' 'poster poems,' an embroidered poem of Philippe Soupault, a Mayakovsky hanging on the wall.

What seems to have intrigued Sonia in particular was alphabet play with shapes and colors, which, like Rimbaud in his famous sonnet 'Les Voyelles,' she assigned to vowels and consonants as well. In fact the impact of Rimbaud upon her work seems to have preceded the influence on Robert, whose watercolor based on excerpts from Rimbaud dates from 1914.

Letter play was to remain a constant in Sonia's *oeuvre*. In 1947 she did a study for the letter *A* in gouache and crayon in which the initial letter *A*

of the *Marseillaise* figures prominently. In 1953 she did the illustrations in color for an edition of Rimbaud's *Illuminations*. In her 1954 testimonial to Cendrars (see above) it was only natural for her to recall above all the 'Prose du Transsibérien . . . ' and her binding of *Les Pâques a New York* (which might well be called a 'poem-poem'), but there were other instances of her collaboration with Cendrars at roughly the same time.

There was, for example, the Zenith series. In August 1913 Cendrars sent Sonia a short poem that he had dashed off on a call slip at the Bibliothèque Mazarine, where he was copying incunabula for Apollinaire. Sonia began playing with the letters and produced a series of variations collectively entitled 'Zenith' after the principal word of each text (see above). Since Zenith is also the name of a watch, it has been assumed that Sonia was creating advertising posters. This may well have been the case, but this suggestion of commercial art should in no way detract from the quality of the poem.

If we compare a printed version, with its free-verse lines, black on white, with the colored lettering of Sonia Delaunay, we discover complications and ambiguities in the latter that make it almost a separate poem (see plate 6). The word 'Zenith,' for example, a mere title in the Cendrars version, becomes of paramount importance, its large characters cutting obliquely as they do from the top towards the bottom. In the upper triangle the letter *Z*, having become, through a reversal in the alphabet, the sign of culmination (*Z* for 'Zenith'), stands alive in its greenness alongside an *O* that Sonia Delaunay has added, which in the context can be read as a representation of the white sun at high noon (unless it is an exclamation!). This *O* in turn stands as a synonym of a different color for the caption that underlies it: 'Midi,' printed in red as the color of fire. The main verb, 'Bat,' also in red, carries us across the zenith dividing line to the prepositional phrase and the direct object, which do not differ essentially from the last lines of the Cendrars version, except that by painting 'solaire' and 'les Rayons' in the same hue of red that connects them with the subject ('Midi Bat') the artist has intensified the degree of heat already generated by the words of the original text. Note finally that in the colored version all the letters stand without exception against a black background—the black of outer space?

In any case the manuscript may be Cendrars's, but it is the colors and shapes that fashion this poem in its finished form and that fully justify placing Sonia Delaunay-Terk among the poets of this anthology.

PAUL DERMÉE

6.

Agrafes d'Argent

Tu te bandes comme un arc

LA BÊTE qu'il faudrait tuer
pince joyeusement la harpe
      Chantez nerfs   gorge criez

Dans une eau chaude et verdâtre
      lentement glisse
           Un geste un soupir une plainte
           vont irriter ses dents sauvages

L'oreille ouverte
      rien ne bouge
Un cri
      voilà qu'un vent tranchant
fait tomber les brandons pourpres
      Vole la flamme   allume la joue

Une table pour s'accouder
      le froid
      la montre   ciseaux à broder
      la couverture sur ses épaules tièdes

Est-ce un monde en formation
      qui tourne en sifflant tout au fond de mon être

Silver Clasps

You tense up like a bow

From
Nord-Sud, nos. 6–7
(August–September
1917), 7.

THE BEAST that must be killed
gaily plucks the harp
   Sing nerves   throat cry

In a hot greenish body of water
     slowly slides
       A gesture a sigh a moan
       will provoke his wild teeth

The ear open

     nothing moves

A cry

    and there a cutting wind
makes the purple firebrands fall
     Steal the flame   light the cheek

A table to lean the elbow on
  the cold
     the watch   embroidery scissors
   the cover on his tepid shoulders

Is it a world in the making
  that turns as it whistles to the depths of my being

Il brûle
S'il allait apparaître
Rosaire sanglant à la fenêtre
soleil couchant sur les marais

LA BÊTE MORD
Voussure
Contracte le silence
Ferme les yeux pour passer le gué

```
                                    V
A       Je la piétine avec une ineffable rage   I
                                              C
h       Chant de triomphe                  T
                                         O
!                 sur mon ennemi vaincu  I
                                          R
                                           E
```

L'holocauste monte en spirales.

It is burning

        Suppose it were to appear

A bleeding rosary at the window

            a sun setting on the marshlands

THE BEAST BITES

       Arching

         Contract the silence

Close your eyes to pass the ford

                  V

A   I stamp on it with unutterable rage   I

                   C

h   Song of triumph   T

                  O

!   on my vanquished enemy R

                    Y

The holocaust rises in spirals

Poème

As de pique

                        ce verre

                                la cendre de la pipe

Bougie éteinte plantée sur mes amours

                              Matin pluvieux

      et cet ennui qui pèse

Le jeu de cartes où rêve l'avenir

Poem

Ace of spades

                    this glass

                            the ash from the pipe

Candle gone out planted on my loves

                          Rainy morning

      and that boredom that weighs

The card game in which the future dreams

From *Nord-Sud*, no. 11 (January 1918), 5.

Poème

Est-ce un avion dans le ciel
                                une abeille

O Souvenir tu chantes dans ma pensée
Rose blanche
                ton rire
                        l'ombrelle verte

Un papillon butine l'herbe
La carpe saute au ruisseau d'acier
Ma cigarette dans les arbres
                                air de flûte
Soleil   ma tête bourdonne

Cette basse éternelle à l'horizon
                        est-ce la chute d'eau
                                ou le canon

Poem

Is it a plane in the sky
                    a bee

From *Nord-Sud*, no. 8
(October 1917), 12.

Oh Memory you sing in my thought
White rose
              your laughter
                        the green parasol

A butterfly gathers the grass
The carp jumps in the steely brook
My cigarette in the trees
                        an air on the flute
Sun   my head buzzes

This constant basso on the horizon
                    is it the waterfall
                          or the cannon

Deux Poèmes

I

Moulin à café

le vent au travers

Les ailes de ton nez frémissent

Un rythme lent

Romance

Le ciel tourne

Une roue

Ces lettres sous la porte

Une vie nouvelle

Guerre lointaine

Et mon verre qui fume

Une clarté couronne l'univers

Two Poems

I

From *Nord-Sud*, no. 12
(February 1918), 6–7.

Coffee grinder

        the wind across

     The wings of your nose quiver

       A slow rhythm

       Romance

       The sky turns

         A wheel

Those letters under the door

       A new life

       The war at a distance

       And my drinking glass that smokes

A brightness crowns the universe

II

Ces pommes

           et la blancheur du compotier

La pointe du couteau a fait une blessure

Ton linge soulevé

      le sein paraît

          La lune

Des lèvres

      Mon désir nocturne se ranime

■

Poème

Je joue à la paume avec les obus.
Sur le bord du chemin

              si pâle

Madame

    Le portrait est crevé d'une étoile de sang
Pleure ton amant

        qui ne reviendra plus

II

These apples

          and the whiteness of the bowl

The tip of the knife has made a wound

Your underlinen raised

        the breast appears

           The moon

Lips

        My nocturnal desire revives

■

Poem

I play tennis with the shells.
On the side of the road

                so pale

Madame

    The portrait is split with a star of blood

Weep for your lover

        who will never return

From *SIC*, nos. 19–20
(July–August 1917), 152.

Paul Dermée

Paul Dermée was the pen name of Camille Janssen (1886–1951), who was born in Liège, Belgium. After university studies in Belgium he settled in Montmartre, where he became closely associated with Juan Gris, Max Jacob, and Pierre Reverdy. For the first issue of Reverdy's avant-garde review *Nord-Sud*, in March 1917, Dermée wrote an essay titled 'Quand le symbolisme fut mort' (After Symbolism's death), which in effect announced the birth of literary cubism. Apollinaire wrote to congratulate Dermée on what he called 'le manifeste de *Nord-Sud*,' and Dermée was to go on speaking of a 'new aesthetic' that owed its origins to the joint influence of two very different nineteenth-century poets, Rimbaud and Mallarmé.

From the first issue, Dermée became the number-two man of *Nord-Sud*, successfully steering it through crises brought on by the more volatile Reverdy. Dermée contributed a score of poems and essays to the magazine at the same time that he collaborated with *SIC*. They illustrate more or less successfully some of the theories expressed in Dermée's manifesto—the notion of the poem as an autonomous object, the rapprochement on the page of disparate realities, the rejection of narrative and descriptive poetry, the fracturing of syntax, the stress on the instantaneous.

Dermée's earliest volumes of poetry were published with illustrations by fellow cubists: Henri Laurens for *Spirales* (1917), Juan Gris for *Beautés de 1918* (Beauties of 1918) (1919), and Louis Marcoussis for *Le Volant d'Artimon* (Wheel of Artimon) (1922). A *papier collé* by Gris (see plate 8) is noteworthy for its fusion of a series of geometric figures with the printed text of Dermée's 'Poème' ['As de pique . . . '], which had originally appeared in *Nord-Sud*. Certain fragments, such as the bottom part of an ace of spades, and the central position of a goblet invite the reader-viewer to connect the two media.

Paul Dermée's wife, the Rumanian Caroline Goldstein, represents the progression from cubism to dadaism. Writing under the name Céline Arnauld, she was a regular contributor to the postwar periodical *L'Esprit nouveau* (New spirit), whose name was borrowed from Apollinaire, and various dadaist publications.

7.

PIERRE DRIEU LA ROCHELLE

Tennis

Clarté nue
Blancheurs qui s'enlèvent
Lignes

Terre tapée tassée tendue qui repousse le pied qui la frappe avec
l'allégresse du tambour
Terre tangible évidence volumineuse
Muscle ramassé à plein sous le talon comme la poitrine du boxeur

Sol épilé glabre Élégance stérile
Blancheur du papier écartelé à quatre pointes sur la table sérénité
offerte à la décision du dessinateur
Le trait clôt le lieu
Dans le trait fermé dans la mesure marquée le corps se décoche, se
suspend
Il est cueilli
Ici tout l'excès est lâché et retenu L'homme châtie sa
force
La détente outrée de la balle l'éclatement blanc est restreint par les
nattes de fer qui mesurent le ciel

L'homme est confiné dans le vain exercice
Une sagesse joyeuse enclôt la jeune troupe dans ses claires-voies
Voici le lieu conquis

Tennis

Naked clarity
Whitenesses that strip off
Lines

From *Fond de Cantine*
(Within the canteen)
(1920), in *Écrits de jeun-
esse* (Youthful writings)
(Paris: Gallimard, 1941),
87–88.

Earth tapped compressed stretched that pushes back the foot that
strikes it with all the liveliness of a drum
Tangible earth voluminous evidence
Muscle fully gathered in beneath the heel like the chest of a boxer

Earth plucked clean-shaven Elegance all sterile
Whiteness of the paper stretched to four tips on the table serenity
offered to the decision of the draughtsman
The stroke closes the spot
In the closed stroke in the marked measure the body lets fly, hangs
in midair
It is picked up
Here all the excess is released and held back The Man punishes his
strength
The excessive relaxation of the ball the white burst is restrained by
the metal matting which measures the sky

Man is confined in the vain exercise
A joyous wisdom encloses the young troop within its gratings
This is the conquered place

Une figure sous le pied prescrit une danse
La ligne lie l'élan
Le rythme se compose des bonds profus et brefs
Modestie du corps athlétique qui se contente de sa
perfection
Tu pourrais borner ton existence humaine à remplir d'un muscle ta
forme

Voici le jeu
O noble hilarité

La courbe sèche d'une vierge orne l'angle infligé à l'espace
Un point en son corps rallie les lignes

A figure under the foot prescribes a dance
The line binds the elan
The rhythm is composed by a profusion of quick jumps
The modesty of the athletic body which is contented with its
perfection
You could limit your human existence to filling your shape with a
muscle

Here is the game
Oh noble hilarity

The dry curve of a virgin adorns the angle inflicted upon space
A point on her body rallies the lines.

Rondeur

> . . . Chant

Que tout notre air soit criblé des radieuses incantations.

Qu'aux récepteurs loquaces le mot de la communion
crépite comme les baisers d'une rencontre

Que la dernière nouvelle frappe au front les foules
nocturnes

Une sentence brève parcourt les façades ondoyantes

Les lettres attendaient dans l'ombre de toute éternité

Un serpent de feu coule par leurs veines invisibles et
s'évade

Que dans le chaos noir où se brouillent les mers et les
ciels les projecteurs embouchent leurs blanches trompettes
de silence

Que les sirènes hurlent la plainte des déesses traquées

Parmi les foules s'effeuillent les journaux

> Dernière Nouvelle
> Le Terre est prise

La Terre est ronde dans la main de l'homme

La maturité a gagné toute la rondeur

Fruit pelé dans la bouche

Une présence d'esprit est dans tous les lieux

Roundness

... Chant

From *Fond de Cantine*,
in *Écrits de jeunesse*,
98–99.

Let all our air be riddled with radiant incantations.

On the loquacious receivers let the word of the communion
crackle like the kisses of a chance meeting

Let the latest news strike the nocturnal crowds on
the brow

A brief maxim runs across the wavy façades

The letters waited in the shadow of all eternity

A fiery serpent flows through their invisible veins and
escapes

In the black chaos where the seas and the skies become
confused let the projectors blow their white trumpets
of silence

Let the sirens utter their moan of tracked-down goddesses

Amidst the crowds the newspapers shed their leaves

Late News
The Earth is taken

The Earth is round in the hand of man
Ripeness has yielded all the roundness
Peeled fruit in the mouth
A presence of mind is everywhere

Géométrie nerveuse

Les lignes de la sphère sont sensibles comme les fibres

qui vont jusqu'au bord du corps

Les méridiens caparaçonnent mes épaules

L'équateur est ma ceinture

Je sens mon frère antipodique

Je sens la plante de ses pieds . . .

Geometry of nerves
The lines of the sphere are sensitive like the fibers
that go to the edge of the body
The meridians caparison my shoulders
The equator is my belt
I perceive my brother of the antipodes
I feel the soles of his feet . . .

Pierre Drieu La Rochelle

Pierre Drieu La Rochelle (1893–1945) is known primarily as the Second World War collaborator who espoused fascism and who committed suicide with the defeat of the Nazis. He is less well known as a collaborator with *SIC* back in 1917. His first volume of poems, *Interrogations* (1917), comprising war poems for the most part—Drieu was wounded at the battle of Charleroi—was favorably reviewed for *SIC* by Pierre Albert-Birot with the reservation that it tended to be too 'philosophical.' There also appeared in *SIC* a description of a matinée in which the poetry of Drieu was recited along with pieces by Apollinaire, Albert-Birot, Paul Dermée, and others.[1] The excerpt from 'Rondeur' above originally appeared in *SIC* under the title 'Dernière Nouvelle' (Read all about it!), along with 'Usine' (Factory).

The war poems have been characterized by Dominique Desanti as poems of violence 'where the rhythm recalls Claudel, the imagery Rimbaud and the thought Nietzsche.'[2]

A second volume of poems, *Fond de Cantine* (Within the canteen), containing such titles as 'Jazz,' 'Secteur américain,' 'T.S.F.' (Wireless telegraphy), 'Vengeance,' and 'Revolution,' appeared in 1920. Drieu read his 'T.S.F.' at a soirée given by the patron of the avant-garde Paul Poiret

1. 'Sic Ambulant,' *SIC*, no. 15 (March 1917).

2. *Drieu La Rochelle: Le séducteur mystifié* (Paris: Flammarion, 1978).

during the war. It reminds one at times of Apollinaire and Cendrars, but by and large Drieu's style is closer to the rhetorical style of Claudel's *Cinq grandes Odes* (Five grand odes) than to the style of the cubists. In the excerpt from 'Rondeur' above, the piling up of the hortatory clauses introduced by 'Que' creates an effect more like that of the traditional Pindaric ode than, for example, Cocteau's *L'ode à Picasso*. 'Tennis' (see above) may be somewhat more restrained, but even there a line such as 'O noble hilarité' has a Nietzschean ring. (Drieu, it seems, had bought a copy of *Also Sprach Zarathustra* [Thus spake Zarathustra] when he was fourteen.) Most of the cubists knew their Nietzsche well, but they also knew that poetry and ideologies rarely mix. In any case, from 1920 on Drieu La Rochelle gave up poetry for fiction and the prose essay.

CHARLOTTE GARDELLE

8.

L'Air

Etre couché au dessus
de la route des hommes
Près d'un boeuf antique
porteur d'eau
Paroles de l'herbe—horizons
Villes bouquets—lacs—derrière les monts
Piémont—France
Malaise du bien être
La jeunesse des sapins
Le mont rose tous les glaciers
L'air
Campo di fiori!
Campo di fiori!

Poèmes

Pluie

O pluie aimable
Laveuse d'arbres
et de toits
qui les a préparés
pour
le rayon rose
du soir

Dimanche tranquille

Mon ami dort
Je lis Ovide
Et tout à l'heure
Je peindrai un petit ornement
Jaune
sur des socques vertes

Air

Lying above
   the road of men
Near an ancient ox
   water-carrier
Speech of the grass—horizons
Cities bouquets—lakes—behind the Alps
      Piedmont—France
Uneasiness of well-being
The youth of the fir trees
The pink mountain all the glaciers
    air
        Campo di fiori!
        Campo di fiori!

From *SIC*, nos. 40–41
(February–March 1919),
329; 44 (April 1919), 362.

Poems

Rain

Oh amiable rain
Washer of trees
and roofs
who has prepared them
for
the pink ray
of evening

Peaceful Sunday

My lover is asleep
I am reading Ovid
And in a moment
I shall paint a little adornment
Yellow
on green clogs

Charlotte Gardelle

Charlotte Gardelle was born in Romania of French parents in 1879. After studying at the Académie Julien in Paris, she annually submitted works— landscapes, still lifes, scenes of the Midi and the Mediterranean—to the Salon d'Automne, from the time of its founding in 1903. According to Apollinaire, she was one of the signers in 1913 of a protest to the police criticizing the banning of a Kees Van Dongen work from the Salon purely on moral grounds.

In 1916 *SIC* announced a Gardelle show in the gallery of Berthe Weill, one of the earliest art dealers to sympathize with the cubists. In her memoirs Weill describes Gardelle's work as 'elegant' as well as 'decorative,' adding, 'Why should that word be pejorative?'[1]

At approximately the same time *SIC* published several of Gardelle's poems (see above). 'L'Air' has a fairly modest typographical arrangement in comparison with the poems of Cocteau, say, or Dermée. On a first reading one is struck by the position of the last two lines, set off as they are from all the other lines, which seem to be in an atmosphere enclosed between the title word 'L'Air' and its repetition at the end. Why are the last two lines written in Italian? And why are there exclamation marks in a text otherwise as free of punctuation as Apollinaire's *Alcools*? Upon

1. *Pan! dans l'Oeil!* (Paris: Librairie Lipshutz, 1933), 210–11.

further readings one gradually senses that all the disparate elements of the enumeration come together to evoke not merely a static Alpine landscape but the crossing of it to the plains below. One is entering not only a new topography but a new country, more ancient (as suggested in the opening lines), and a new language. And the joy of that arrival is intensified by the exclamation marks and the repetition of the closing phrase.

If we may judge from their regular syntax, the two little 'Poems' of Gardelle are not cubist. Their charm lies in their brevity and their simplicity. 'Dimanche tranquille,' if it were not for the anachronism, could almost pass for a fragment from Sappho.

VICENTE HUIDOBRO

9.

Nouvelle Chanson
Pour Toi, Manuelita

En dedans de l'Horizon
QUELQU'UN CHANTAIT

          Sa voix
       N'est pas connue
             D'OU VIENT-IL

Parmi les branches
On ne voit personne

La lune même était une oreille

Et on n'entend
          aucun bruit

          Cependant
               une étoile déclouée
Est tombée dans l'étang

       L'HORIZON
           S'EST FERME

Et il n'y a pas de sortie

New Song
For You, Manuelita

Inside the Horizon

SOMEONE WAS SINGING

> The voice

> Is not known

WHERE DOES IT COME FROM

Among the branches
No one is to be seen

The moon itself was an ear

And one hears

> no sound

> However

> a star unnailed

Has fallen into the pond

THE HORIZON

HAS CLOSED UP

And there is no exit

From
*Obras completas de
Vicente Huidobro*, vol. 1,
Horizon carré (Square
horizon) (Santiago: Zig-
Zag, 1963), 261–62.

Aveugle

Au delà de la dernière fenêtre
Les cloches du Sacré-Coeur
Font tomber les feuilles

SUR LE SOMMET

UN AVEUGLE

Les paupières pleines de musique
Lève les mains

au milieu du vide

Celle qui vient de loin
Ne lui a pas donné son bras

Il est tout seul

Et avec sa gorge coupée

Il chante une mélodie

que personne

n'a comprise

Blind

Beyond the last window
The bells of the Sacré-Coeur
Make the leaves fall

From
*Obras completas de
Vicente Huidobro*, vol. 1,
Horizon carré, 264–65.

ON THE SUMMIT

A BLIND MAN

Eyelids full of music
Raises his hands
            in the midst of the void

She who comes from afar
Has not given him her arm

He is all alone

            And with his broken voice

He sings a melody
            that no one
                        has understood

Minuit

Les heures glissent
Comme des gouttes d'eau sur une vitre

                              Silence de minuit

La peur se déroule dans l'air
Et le vent
            se cache au fond du puits

                    OH

            C'est une feuille
                On pense que la terre va finir
                Le temps
                          remue dans l'ombre

Tout le monde dort

                UN SOUPIR

Dans la maison quelque'un vient de mourir

Midnight

The hours glide
Like drops of water on a window pane

From
*Obras completas de
Vicente Huidobro*, vol. 1,
Horizon carré, 265.

         Midnight silence

Fear unrolls in the air
And the wind
      hides at the bottom of the well

    OH

   It's a leaf
     We think the earth is going to end
    Time
       stirs in the shadow

Everyone is asleep

    A SIGH

Inside the house someone has just died

Matin

SOLEIL

Qui réveille Paris

SOLEIL

Le plus haut peuplier de la rive

Sur la Tour Eiffel
Un coq á trois couleurs
Chante en battant des ailes
Et quelques plumes en tombant

SOLEIL

En recommençant sa course
La Seine chereche entre les ponts
Sa vieille route

Et l'Obélisque
Qui a oublié les mots égyptiens
N'a pas fleuri cette année

SOLEIL

Morning

SUN

That awakens Paris

From *Obras completas ce*
Vicencente Huidobro,
vol.1, Horizon carrEe, 282

On the Eiffel Tower

A tricolored cock

SUN

The highest poplar on the bank

Sings to the flapping of his wings

And several feathers fall

SUN

As it resumes its course

The Seine looks between the bridges

For her old route

And the Obelisk

That has forgotten the Egyptian words

Has not blossomed this year

SUN

Tour Eiffel

A Robert Delaunay

Tour Eiffel
Guitare du ciel

      Ta télégraphie sans fil
      Attire les mots
      Comme un rosier les abeilles

Pendant la nuit
La Seine ne coule plus

      Télescope ou clairon

TOUR EIFFEL

Et c'est une ruche de mots
Ou un encrier de miel

Au fond de l'aube
Une araignée aux pattes en fil de fer
Faisait sa toile de nuages

      Mon petit garçon
      Pour monter à la Tour Eiffel
      On monte sur une chanson

Eiffel Tower

To Robert Delaunay

From
Poesía y prosa,
201–3.

Eiffel Tower
Guitar of the sky

       Your wireless telegraphy
       Attracts words
       As a rosebush the bees

During the night
The Seine no longer flows

       Telescope or bugle

     EIFFEL TOWER

And it's a hive of words
Or an inkwell of honey

At the bottom of dawn
A spider with barbed-wire legs
Was making its web of clouds

       My little boy
       To climb the Eiffel Tower
       You climb on a song

Do
ré
mi
fa
`
sol
la
si
do

Nous sommes en haut

Un oiseau chante   C'est le vent
Dans les antennes   De l'Europe
Télégraphiques   Le vent électrique

Là-bas

Les chapeaux s'envolent
Ils ont des ailes mais ils ne chantent pas

Jacqueline
          Fille de France
Qu'est-ce que tu vois là-haut

La Seine dort
Sous l'ombre de ses ponts

Je vois tourner la Terre
Et je sonne mon clairon

Do
 re
  mi
   fa
    sol
     la
      ti
       do

We are up on top

A bird sings   It's the wind
in the telegraph   Of Europe
antennae   The electric wind

             Over there

The hats fly away
They have wings but they don't sing

Jacqueline
             Daughter of France
What do you see up there

The Seine is asleep
Under the shadow of its bridges

I see the Earth turning
And I blow my bugle

Vers toutes les mers

> Sur le chemin
> De ton parfum
> Tous les abeilles et les paroles s'en vont

> Sur les quatre horizons
Qui n'a pas entendu cette chanson

JE SUIS LA REINE DE L'AUBE DES POLES

JE SUIS LA ROSE DES VENTS QUI SE FANE TOUS LES
     AUTOMNES

ET TOUTE PLEINE DE NEIGE

JE MEURS DE LA MORT DE CETTE ROSE

DANS MA TETE UN OISEAU CHANTE TOUTE L'ANNEE

C'est comme ça qu'un jour la Tour m'a parlé

Tour Eiffel
  Volière du monde
          Chante   Chante
Sonnerie de Paris

Le géant pendu au milieu du vide
Est l'affiche de France

> Le jour de la Victoire
> Tu la raconteras aux étoiles

Toward all the seas

> On the path
> Of your perfume
> All the bees and the words go their way

> On the four horizons

Who has not heard this song

I AM THE QUEEN OF THE DAWN OF THE POLES

I AM THE COMPASS THE ROSE OF THE WINDS THAT FADES

    EVERY FALL

AND ALL FULL OF SNOW

I DIE FROM THE DEATH OF THAT ROSE

IN MY HEAD A BIRD SINGS ALL YEAR LONG

That's the way the Tower spoke to me one day

Eiffel Tower
   Aviary of the world
                Sing   Sing
Chimes of Paris

The giant hanging in the midst of the void
Is the poster of France

> The day of Victory
> You will tell it to the stars

Vicente Huidobro

Born in Santiago de Chile into an old Spanish family in 1893, Vicente Huidobro received an education that looked to Europe, especially Spain and France. He arrived in Paris at the end of 1916 and while still a student allied himself with the cubists. With Reverdy, Huidobro helped to found the review *Nord-Sud*. Although only four years Huidobro's senior, Reverdy acted as his mentor, translating his early work and guiding him towards the cubist style. Indeed it is at times difficult to distinguish between the two. They were kindred souls, and it is a pity that their squabbles over the authorship of their theories—they both loved to theorize—generated so much bitterness.

Huidobro contributed a dozen pieces to *Nord-Sud*,[1] several of which he included in his first French-language volume, *Horizon carré* (Square horizon), in 1917.[2] Except for 'Tour Eiffel,' the poems above are taken from this volume. The affinities with Reverdy are evident: a sense of all-enveloping disquiet and mystery with enigmatic events taking place in an anonymous world. The first piece, 'Nouvelle Chanson,' ends with a line that says in effect 'No exit.' In 'Minuit' someone—'quelqu'un'—has just died. 'Aveugle' contains a melody that no one has understood. And so on.

The title of this volume is based on an image (square horizon) that

1. *Nord-Sud*, nos. 2–10 (April–December 1917).

2. Volume 1 of *Obras completas de Vicente Huidobro* (Santiago: Zig-Zag, 1963).

Huidobro makes the basis of his entire aesthetic. Alluding to a volume Reverdy had published a year earlier (1916), *Lucarne oval* (Oval skylight), Huidobro wrote boastfully: 'While others were making oval skylights I was making square horizons.' Since all skylights are oval, poetry continues to be realist; since horizons are not square, the author offers something created by himself. This notion of the poem as an autonomous object Huidobro baptized 'creationism.' It was a concept that—and he would have been loath to admit this—not only goes back at least as far as Baudelaire but was shared by cubist poets and painters alike, Reverdy most of all.

Huidobro's originality lies less in his aesthetic theories as such than in the images they generate. When he wrote, for instance, that thanks to the adjective 'square,' something as vast as the horizon is 'humanized,' he was in effect preparing the way for the opening image of his 'Tour Eiffel': 'guitare du ciel.' In 'Tour Eiffel' one finds an effort at humanization similar to that Apollinaire sought in his 'Bergère o Tour Eiffel . . . ' of 'Zone.' Or when again in 'Tour Eiffel' Huidobro writes 'Et c'est une ruche de mots / Ou un encrier de miel,' he is illustrating his belief that the poet should achieve a balance between the abstract and the concrete (*encrier de mots* and *ruche de miel*).

The image of the square horizon furthermore suggests a framing process that may be reflected in the shape of the poem, its typographical arrangement. Note, for example, 'Matin,' where the word SOLEIL (sun), in capital letters, appears on all four sides of the text, simultaneously enclosing and illuminating the verbal landscape. It was undoubtedly such framing that led Huidobro to his 'painted poems,' which he exhibited in Paris in 1922.

After the publication of his final work in French, *Tout à coup* (All of a sudden) (1925), Huidobro returned to South America, where he was known at the time of his death (1948) as one of the major Latin American poets of the twentieth century. His cubist phase did not count for naught towards this.

MAX JACOB

10.

Le Coq et la Perle

❖

Ses bras blancs devinrent tout mon horizon.

❖

Un incendie est une rose sur la queue ouverte d'un paon

❖

Il était deux heures du matin : elles étaient élégantes les trois vieilles, comme on l'eût été il y a cinquante ans ; châles de dentelles noires, bonnets à brides, camées, robes de soie noire marquant les plis de l'étoffe fabriquée. Le trottoir était désert et leurs yeux gros de larmes se levaient vers une fenêtre dont le rideau était faiblement éclairé.

❖

Augustine était fille de ferme quand le Président la remarqua. Pour éviter le scandale, il lui décerna des titres et des brevets d'institutrice, puis un 'de' vers son nom, quelque argent, et plus il la pour-voyait, plus elle était digne de lui. Je me suis tout donné à moi-même, pauvre paysan breton, le titre de duc, le droit de porter un monocle, j'ai pu grandir ma taille, ma pensée et je ne pourrai pas être digne de moi-même.

❖

Il arrive quand tu ronfles que le monde matériel éveille l'autre.

❖

The Rooster and the Pearl

❖

Her white arms became my entire horizon.

❖

A fire is a rose on the open tail of a peacock.

❖

It was two o'clock in the morning: they were elegant those three old ladies, as one might have been fifty years ago; shawls with black lace, beribboned bonnets, cameos, black silk dresses showing the folds of the fabric. The sidewalk was deserted and their eyes, heavy with tears, turned upwards toward a window that had a dimly lighted curtain.

❖

Augustine was a farm girl when the President noticed her. To avoid any scandal he awarded her with titles and teaching certificates, then a 'de' in her name, some money, and the more he bestowed upon her the more she became worthy of him. I've given myself everything, poor peasant of Brittany, the title of duke, the right to wear a monocle. I've been able to increase my height, my mind, and I shall not be worthy of myself.

❖

It happens when you snore that the material world awakens the other.

❖

From
Le Cornet à dés (The dice cup) (Paris: Gallimard, 1945), 51–54, 56, 60, 66. The title is borrowed from La Fontaine's *Fables* (1 and 20).

En descendant la rue de Rennes, je mordais dans mon pain avec tant d'émotion qu'il me sembla que c'était mon coeur que je déchirais.

Pour montrer l'importance su service de bouche chez les Rothschild, un magazine a représenté cette famille en petit au bas d'une pile énorme d'assiettes. Un lecteur examine les fourmis avec une loupe :
     'Lequel est Henri? lequel est Henri?'

L'enfant, l'éfant, l'éléphant, la grenouille et la pomme sautée.

Autour de la baie, au nord, au sud, habitent derrière chaque rocher un frère ou une soeur de Napoléon.

Comme un bateau est le poète âgé
ainsi qu'un dahlia, le poème étagé
Dahlia! Dahlia! que Dalila lia.

Un diadème est changé en mille têtes de députés.

Going down the Rue de Rennes I would bite into my loaf of bread with so much emotion that it seemed to me it was my heart I was tearing apart.

❖

To show the importance of the cuisine at the Rothschilds' a magazine pictured the family on a reduced scale at the foot of an enormous pile of plates. One reader examines the ants with a magnifying glass:
'Which one is Henri? which one is Henri?'

❖

The infant, the efant, the elephant, the frog and the fried potato.

❖

Around the bay, to the north, to the south, there lives behind each rock a brother or a sister of Napoleon.

❖

Like a boat is the poet aged
just like a dahlia, the poem stacked
Dahlia! Dahlia! by Delilah bound.

❖

A diadem is changed into a thousand deputy heads.

Petit Poème

Je me souviens de ma chambre d'enfant. La mousseline des rideaux sur la vitre était griffonée de passementeries blanches, je m'efforçais d'y retrouver l'alphabet et quand je tenais les lettres, je les transformais en dessins que j'imaginais. H, un homme assis ; B, l'arche d'un pont sur un fleuve. Il y avait dans la chambre plusieurs coffres et des fleurs ouvertes sculptées légèrement sur le bois. Mais ce que je préférais, c'était deux boules de pilastres qu'on apercevait derrière les rideaux et que je considérais comme des têtes de pantins avec lesquels il était défendu de jouer.

Little Poem

I remember my childhood bedroom. The muslin of the curtains on the pane was scrawled with white trimmings, I would make every effort to locate the alphabet and when I held the letters I would change them into designs that I would imagine. *H*, a seated man; *B*, the arch of a bridge over a river. In the room there were several chests with flowers in bloom lightly sculptured on the wood. But what I preferred was the two pilaster balls that one could see behind the curtains and that I took to be puppet heads that it was forbidden to play with.

From
Le Cornet à dés, 155.

Générosité Espagnole

Par un Espagnol de mes amis, le roi d'Espagne m'a fait donner trois gros diamants sur une chemise, une collerette de dentelle sur une veste de toréador, un portefeuille contenant des recommandations sur la conduite de la vie. Voitures! boulevards, visites chez des amis : la bonne couchera-t-elle avec moi? M. S. L. a tendu la main à G. A. qui la lui a refusée sans motifs. Je suis raccommodé avec les Y . . . Or, voici qu'à la Bibliothèque Nationale je m'aperçois que je suis surveillé. Quatre employés s'avancent vers moi avec une épée de poupée chaque fois que je cherche à lire certains livres. Enfin un tout jeune groom s'avance : 'Venez!' me dit-il. Il me montre un puits caché derrière les livres ; il me montre une roue de planches qui a l'air d'un instrument de supplices : 'Vous lisez des livres sur l'Inquisition, vous êtes condamné à mort!' et je vis que sur ma manche on avait brodé une tête de mort: 'Combien? dis-je. — Combien pouvez-vous donner? — Quinze francs. C'est trop, dit le groom. — Je vous les donnerai lundi.' La générosité du roi d'Espagne avait attiré l'attention de l'Inquisition. . . .

Le corbeau d'Edgar Poe a une auréole qu'il éteint parfois.

❖

Le pauvre examine le manteau de saint Martin et dit : 'Pas de poches?'

❖

Adam et Ève sont nés à Quimper.

Spanish Generosity

Thanks to a Spanish friend of mine the king of Spain had given me three large diamonds on a shirt, a lace collar on a toreador jacket, a portfolio containing recommendations on how to live. Carriages! boulevards, visits to friends: will the maid sleep with me? M.S.L. offered her hand to G.A. who refused it for no reason at all. I have made up with the Ys. . . . Now suddenly at the Bibliothèque Nationale I realize that I am being watched. Four employees approach me with puppet swords each time I try to read certain books. Finally a very young page steps forward: 'Come,' he tells me. He shows me a well hidden behind the books; he shows me a wheel with planks that looks like a torture machine: 'You are reading books on the Inquisition, you are condemned to death!' and I saw that on my sleeve someone had embroidered a skull. 'How much?' I asked – How much can you give? – Fifteen francs. – 'That's too much,' said the page. – 'I'll give them to you on Monday.' The generosity of the king of Spain had attracted the attention of the Inquisition. . . .

The raven of Edgar Allen Poe has a halo that he extinguishes from time to time.

❖

The poor man examines Saint Martin's cloak and says: 'No pockets?'

❖

Adam and Eve were born in Quimper.

From
Le Cornet à dés, 168.

Honneur de la Sardane et de la Tenora

Dédié à Picasso

Mer est la mer Égée qui dépasse Alicante.
Ah! que n'ai-je vingt-cinq mille livres de rentes!
Les montagnes veillaient sur la mer et la ville.
Sur les murs s'étalait le blason de Castille ;
Des églises carrées et les maisons aussi
Et les gens ont toujours l'air de vous dire merci.
Tous ces Romains seraient de l'Opéra-Comique
Si la toge jamais pouvait être comique.
Bleu de cravates bleues aux forains dépassant.
Si les pruneaux étaient couleur d'olive claire
Ce seraient des pruneaux que ces vieillards sévères,
Ces vieillards sont trop maigres ; trop gros ces jeunes gens!
Les gitanes iront au cinématographe
Les chevreaux futures outres ont des cous de girafes
Des Catalans phrygiens vendaient des escargots
Les tartanes ont courbés des voiles de bateaux
Et les rames étaient les pattes des chevaux.
Qui veut des calamars, des pieuvres, des rascasses?
Ces poissons ont des dents, des lunettes, des masques
Les toits sont en gradin place du Caïman
Les stores, les balcons le sont également

In Honor of the Sardana and the Tenora

Dedicated to Picasso

Sea is the Aegean Sea which goes beyond Alicante.
Ah! why don't I have an income of twenty-five thousand pounds!
The mountains stood guard over the sea and the town.
On the walls were displayed the coat of arms of Castile;
Churches square and the houses too
And the people always seem to be thanking you.
All these Romans would belong to the Opéra-Comique
If the toga could ever be comical.
Blue of blue cravats standing out from the street vendors.
If prunes were light olive colored
Those stern old men would be prunes,
Those old men are too skinny; the young ones too fat!
The gipsies will go to the cinema
The kids on their way to becoming leather bottles have giraffe necks
Phrygian Catalonians were selling snails
The tartans bent down their sails
And the oars were horse feet
Who wants squid, octopus, hogfish?
These fish have teeth, goggles, masks
On Cayman square the roofs rise tier upon tier
Likewise the window-blinds, the balconies

From
La Laboratoire central
(The central laboratory)
(Paris: Gallimard, 1960),
49–66.

Peu de fleurs au marché, mais beaucoup de cerises

Les balcons sont embrouillés ; comme à Venise

Les stores ont l'air de chemise

Et des buissons de roses comme la tour de Pise.

La cuisine espagnole sentait un peu le foin

Mais la salle à manger était vraiment mauresque

Si tu n'as jamais vu l'Espagne

Tu ne sais ce que c'est que ville dans campagne.

C'est couleur chocolat ou mieux café au lait

Ou bien c'est blanc dans des montagnes de minerai.

Si tu n'as jamais vu l'Espagne

— Alfred de Musset l'a dit, pour sûr! —

Tu ne sais ce que c'est qu'un mur

Un mur de couvent a des portes cochères

Il en a par devant, il en a par derrière.

Arcades sous les toits, arcades sur la rue.

Dans la journée la ville est nue.

Beaucoup de gens ici sont cireurs de souliers.

Ils jonglent avec la brosse en vous tenant le pied.

Ça n'empêche que sur la citadelle

Deux fois tronquée l'église domine des tourelles.

Il paraît que la forteresse a des canons

Qui garderaient la route du haut de certain mont.

Les soldats sur la tête ont du cuir en canon

Not many flowers at the market but lots of cherries
The balconies are tangled; as in Venice
The blinds look like shirts.
And rose bushes like the Tower of Pisa.
The Spanish cuisine smelled a bit of hay
But the dining room was really Moorish
If you've never seen Spain
You don't know what a city in the country is like.
It's a chocolate color or better café au lait
Or else it's white in the mountains of ore.
If you've never seen Spain
—Alfred de Musset said so, I'm sure!—
You don't know what a wall is
A monastery wall has portes cochères
It has some in front, it has some behind.
Arcades under the roofs, arcades on the street.
In the daytime the city is bare.
Many people here shine shoes.
They juggle with the brush as they hold your foot.
That doesn't prevent the church from dominating the turrets
On the twice-truncated citadel
It seems that the fortress has cannons
Which would protect the road from the top of a certain mount.
The soldiers wear cannon-shaped leather caps

Devant dix-huit cafés ils boivent des canons
      La mère et la fille
Ont des éventails. Deux moustaches brillent.
      La mère est en noir
Excepté les cafés en Bourse du Travail
Où beaucoup d'hommes sont en blouse de travail
Les démons du Soleil habitaient tout le reste.
On en avait fermé les volets avec soin.

Je me souviendrai toute ma vie de l'instrument de musique qui a nom 'Tenora' ; c'est long comme une clarinette et ça lutterait, affirme un musicien, avec quarante trombones. Le son en est sec comme celui de la cornemuse. J'ai entendu la 'Tenora' à Figueras, ville de la Catalogne, dans un petit orchestre sur la place publique. L'orchestre était composé d'un violoncelle, d'un piston, de cuivres et d'une flûte qui faisait de brefs et charmants soli. On dansait la sardane et avant chaque danse l'orchestre exécutait une longue introduction d'une allure grandiloquente. La déclamation de la 'Tenora' était soutenue par les autres instruments bien serrés l'un contre l'autre. Ce sont les musiciens de la ville qui composent cette admirable musique ; leurs noms sont inconnus en France excepté de la Maison Pathé frères. Ces fabricants de phonographes ne reculent devant aucun sacrifice quand il s'agit, etc . . . Après l'introduction, le rythme de la danse commence ; ce rythme est d'une solidité telle que je ne crois pas qu'on puisse souhaiter davantage : un rythme de polka coupé de silences brusques, de

In front of eighteen cafés they drink their glass of wine
    The mother and the daughter
Have fans. Two moustaches shine.
    The mother is in black
Except the Labor Exchange cafés
Where lots of men are wearing workers' shirts
The demons of the Sun inhabited all the rest.
The shutters had been carefully closed.

I'll remember my whole life the musical instrument with the name 'Tenora'; it's long like a clarinet and could compete, as one musician claims, with forty trombones. It has a dry sound like a bagpipe. I heard the 'Tenora' at Figueras, a city in Catalonia in a small orchestra on the public square. The orchestra was made up of a cello, a cornet, brasses and a flute which played charming little solos. The dance was the sardana and before each dance the orchestra would play a long introduction in a grandiloquent style. The declamation of the 'Tenora' was supported by the other instruments closely pressed together. It is the local musicians that compose this admirable music; their names are unknown in France except by the Pathé Brothers, Inc. These manufacturers of phonographs will shrink from nothing when it is a question of, etc. . . . After the introduction, the rhythm of the dance begins; this rhythm is so solid I can't imagine wishing for more: a polka rhythm interrupted by sudden pauses, long appoggiaturas.

longues fioritures. Il y a dans la musique des sardanes des embrasements qui font penser à la splendeur. La sardane se danse en rond, bras en girandoles et presque immobiles, sauf dans les moments d'embrasement. Vous regarderez les pieds des danseurs qui sont tendus et qui exécutent des grimaces gracieuses. Au centre de la ronde, il y a une autre ronde et, au milieu de cette ronde, une autre; et les mouvements de ces rondes sont les mêmes, mais ne coïncident pas, parce que chaque meneur de ronde n'a pas le même sentiment de la musique. Il y avait plusieurs roses de rondes le soir sur le pavé de la place à Figueras.

Sardane! tu es comme une rose
Et toutes ces jeunes filles sont en rose.
Il n'y a que les maisons qui ne dansent pas,
Et l'on se demande pourquoi.

La musique a fait pleurer nos yeux
La musique ingénue a gêné nos poitrines,
Comme elle a regonflé le cercle grave et joyeux
Chantez! chantez! chantez! tenoras et clarines.

Le peuple serait comme les vagues de la mer
Si la mer était rose et tournait dans la nuit,
Si la nuit était rose, si rose était la mer
Et si la mer était comme les arbres verts.

In the music of the sardanas there are fiery glows that give a sense of
splendor. The sardana is danced in a circle with the arms in girandoles
almost motionless except during the fiery moments. You will look at the
feet of the dancers which are stretched out and perform gracious grimaces.
In the center of the circle there is another circle and in the midst of this one
another; and the movements of these circles are the same but do not coin-
cide because each leader has a different sense of the music. There were sev-
eral round roses that evening on the pavement of the square at Figueras.

Sardana! you are like a rose
And all the maidens are rose-like.
Only the houses are not dancing,
And one wonders why,

The music has brought tears to our eyes
The artless music has cramped our chests,
As it has swollen the grave and joyous circle out again
Sing! sing! sing! tenoras and clarinets.

The people would be like the waves of the sea
If the sea were pink and turned in the night,
If the night were pink, if pink were the sea
And if the sea were like the green trees.

Filles des muletiers, gens qui servez à table
Penchez-vous! jetez-vous des regards adorables,
Et par-dessus les bras tendus en candélabres!
Songez à Dieu qui vous regarde dans les arbres

Et par les yeux des boutiques et par la mer.
La tenora fendait la nuit et sa poussière
Nasillarde, comme avec des éclats de verre
La danse roucoulait noblement avec des passements de pied allègres.

Chaque instrument se tenait par la taille
Et la tenora dans la musique faisait une entaille.

Ainsi que dans une tragédie est un spectre
Qui passe rarement et passe comme un astre
La sèche tenora, trompette nasillarde
Ne bruit que rarement pour de courtes sardanes.

Les fillettes iront se coucher de bonne heure.
Et les hommes seront au café tout à l'heure
Car les musiciens sont payés tant par heure
Quarante pesetas pour donner du bonheur.

Un garçon se plaignait qu'on ne sût plus danser.
Une fille grattait la jambe à son soulier.
Vers la fin, des messieurs et des dames très bien
S'appliquaient du pied gauche et la main dans la main.

Daughters of the muleteers servants at the table
Lean forward! exchange glances of adoration
And above your arms stretched like candelabras!
Think of God who is looking at you in the trees

And through the eyes of the shops and through the sea.
The tenora cut through the night and its dust
Twangy, like bursts of glass
The dance warbles nobly with merry foot trimmings.

Each instrument was held by the waist
And the tenora made a notch in the music.

Just as in a tragedy there is a ghost
Who passes by rarely and passes like a star
The dry tenora, a twangy trumpet,
Sounds only rarely for short sardanas.

The girls will go to bed early
And the men will soon be at the café
For the musicians are paid so much by the hour
Forty pesetas to provide happiness.

A boy was complaining that no one can dance anymore.
A girl was scratching her leg at shoe level
Toward the end, some very proper ladies and gentlemen
Were trying out the left foot hand in hand.

Dansez aussi, dame en grand deuil.
Une fille a reçu de la poussière dans l'oeil.
Elle va se cacher derrière un réverbère
Où l'attendait sa mère avec les autres mères

Et malgré sa douleur elle sourit encore
Aux accents séduisants de l'ardente ténore.
Les balcons se drapaient des couleurs catalanes
Pendant que tressautait la rose des sardanes.

Le choc du jaune et du rouge s'allie assez
Avec, ô tenora, tes gammes alliacées.
Elle m'a grisé comme une eau-de-vie.
Elle s'est éteinte comme une bougie
Son souvenir est dans ma vie.

On dit que l'Empereur a passé par ici
Et qu'on retrouve encor ses soldats dans les puits.
Les soldats ont dansé la sardane en vainqueurs
Couchés derrière ces terrasses, ces géraniums, ces pilastres
Ils ne s'éveillaient plus un poignard dans le coeur.
La sèche tenora a passé comme un astre.

Adieu, sardane et tenora! Adieu, tenoras et sardane
Demain, puisque le sort me damne
Demain puisque le czar l'ordonne

Dance you too, lady in deep mourning.
One girl got some dust in her eyes.
She is going to hide behind a street lamp
Where her mother with other mothers was awaiting her

And in spite of her pain she is still smiling
At the seductive accents of the fiery tenora.
The balconies were draped with the colors of Catalonia
As hopped and jumped the rose of the sardanas.

The shock of yellow and red harmonizes quite well,
Oh tenora, with your garlicky gamuts.
It has intoxicated me like an eau-de-vie
It has gone out like a candle.
Its memory is in my life.

They say the Emperor passed by here
And that one still finds his soldiers in the wells.
As conquerors the soldiers danced the sardana
Sleeping behind these terraces, these geraniums, these pilasters
They woke up no more a dagger in the heart.
The dry tenora has passed by like a star.

Adieu, sardana and tenora! Adieu tenoras and sardana
Tomorrow since fate has condemned me
Tomorrow since the tzar gives the command

Demain je serai loin d'ici
Demain dans les jardins près de ces monastères
Le peuple sourira pour cacher ses prières
Et moi je te dirai merci!

■

Invitation au Voyage

A Louis Bergerot

Les trains! Les trains par les tunnels étreints
Ont fait de ces cabarets roses
Où les tziganes vont leur train
Les tziganes aux valses roses
Des îles chastes de boulingrins.

Il passe sur automobiles
Il passe de fragiles rentières
Comme sacs à loto mobiles.
Vers des parcs aux doux ombrages
Je t'invite ma chère Elise.
Elise! je t'invite au voyage
Vers ces palais de Venise.

Pour cueillir des fleurs aux rameaux
Nous déposerons nos vélos

Tomorrow I'll be far from here
Tomorrow in the gardens near these monasteries
The people will smile to hide their prayers
And I'll say 'Thank you!'

■

Invitation to a Voyage

To Louis Bergerot

The trains! The trains hugged by the tunnels
Have fashioned those pink cabarets
Where the gipsies go their way
The pink-waltz gipsies
Of the virginal bowling-green isles.

On automobiles
The fragile stock-holding ladies go by
Like mobile lotto bags
Toward parks with gentle shade
I invite you my dear Elise.
Elise! I invite you on a voyage
Toward those Venetian palaces.

To pick bough-covered flowers
We'll park our bikes

From
Le Laboratoire central,
189–90.

Devant les armures hostiles
Des grillages modern-style
Nous déposerons nos machines
Pour les décorer d'aubépine
Nous regarderons couler l'eau
En buvant des menthes à l'eau.

Peut-être que sexagénaires
Nous suivrons un jour ces rivières
Dans d'écarlates automates
Dont nous serons propriétaires!
Mais en ces avenirs trop lents
Les chevaux des Panhard
Ne seront-ils volants?

A vendre : quatre véritables déserts
A proximité du chemin de fer,
S'adresser au propriétaire-notaire
M. Chocarneau,
18, boulevard Carnot.

In front of the hostile armor plates
Of the art nouveau grilles of iron.
We'll park our machines
To decorate them with hawthorn
We'll watch the water flow
As we sip cool mint drinks.

Maybe one day in our sixties
We'll go down these rivers
In scarlet automata
Which belong to us!
But in those too long futures
Won't the Panhard horses
Have become air-borne?

For sale: four authentic deserts
Near the railroad,
Contact the owner-notary
M. Chocarneau
18, Boulevard Carnot.

Max Jacob

Max Jacob has described his first meeting with Picasso. In 1901 he had been living in Paris for about five years, having moved from Quimper, in Brittany, where he was born in 1876 of 'Jewish-Voltairean' parents, as he called them. A would-be art critic, he frequented the avant-garde galleries. One day in June he dropped in at Vollard's in the rue Lafitte. There he saw a series of paintings of remarkable originality in spite of the influence of Toulouse-Lautrec and Steinlen. He asked for the name and address of the artist, and the next day he climbed up to the Boulevard Clichy. 'Picasso's French was no better than my Spanish but we looked at each other and shook hands with enthusiasm. That happened in a large studio where a bunch of Spaniards were sitting on the floor, gaily eating and chatting.'[1] The next night at Jacob's, using a kind of sign language, they spoke until dawn. Thus began a friendship that was to last through the cubist period, Jacob's conversion to Catholicism (with Picasso as godfather), and the war. It ended more or less definitively when Jacob withdrew in 1924 to become a recluse in the Abbey of Saint-Benoît-sur-Loire.

It is a fact that Max Jacob 'discovered' Picasso, earlier than Leo and Gertrude Stein, for instance, but he did nothing about it. The first to write

1. 'Souvenirs sur Picasso, contés par Max Jacob,' in *Cahiers d'Art* 6 (1927), 199.

a review of a Picasso exhibit (at the Galeries Serrurier) was Apollinaire, in 1905.[2] In a letter to Jacques Doucet in 1917 Jacob stated categorically: 'I have written nothing on Picasso.' One of the reasons he gives, remarkable in his candor, is that he would not like to be known to posterity as merely 'Picasso's friend.' This meant of course that the collaboration between the two was rather one-sided. Picasso illustrated a number of Jacob's works, but except for the dedication of 'Honneur de la sardane et de la tenora,' Jacob did not reciprocate. It may have been the fear of Picasso's caustic wit. When, for example, their dealer, D. H. Kahnweiler, informed Jacob in 1910 that Picasso had agreed to do a series of etchings for his *Saint Matorel*, etchings that were to become most important in the development of cubist prints, Jacob asked warily, 'But are they serious?' The query was especially apt since Victor Matorel is a thinly disguised, not always flattering portrait of Jacob himself. And had not Picasso already baptized one of the ladies of *Les Demoiselles d'Avignon* 'Mère de Max' (Max's mother)?

Jacob collaborated with Juan Gris but wrote very little on the other cubist painters, limiting his critical writing to poetry and poetics. He was the only one among the poets featured in this volume to attempt a definition of 'literary cubism.' In a 1927 letter to his mother he defines cubism in painting as 'a picture for its own sake.' And he concludes: 'Literary cubism does the same thing in literature, using reality merely as a means and not as an end.'[3]

This definition, based, as was that of Huidobro, on the notion of the

2. *Oeuvres complètes de Guillaume Apollinaire*, ed. Michel Décaudin, 4 vols. (Paris: Balland et Lecat, 1966), 4:64–65.

3. Rare MS., Bibliothèque Nationale, Paris.

autonomy of the work of art (*le tableau-objet*, the painting as object), is so broad as to be useless in its application to literary cubism. It is nonetheless helpful as a clarification of the author's intention. For Jacob the prose poems, the nonsensical aphorisms and anecdotes, the wordplay, the riddles, the surprise endings, and on occasion the deep mysticism— all the varied fragments that make up *Le Cornet à dés*—create in their ensemble a cubist work.

During the Second World War Max Jacob wore the yellow star and died in prison at Drancy in 1944. A punster to the end, he is said to have written, telegraph style: 'Pris par la Gestapo. Prononcez : J'ai ta peau' (Taken by the Gestapo. Pronounce: 'I've got your skin').

MARIE LAURENCIN

11.

Le Présent

Si tu veux je te donnerai
Mon matin, mon matin gai
Avec tous mes clairs cheveux
Que tu aimes ;
Mes yeux verts
Et dorés
Si tu veux.
Je te donnerai tout le bruit
Qui se fait
Quand le matin s'éveille
Au soleil
Et l'eau qui coule
Dans la fontaine
Toute auprès ;
Et puis encore le soir qui viendra vite
Le soir de mon âme triste
A pleurer
Et mes mains toutes petites
Avec mon coeur qu'il faudra près du tien
Garder.

The Present

From Marie Laurencin
[Louise Lalanne, pseud.],
Le Carnet des nuits (The
notebook of the nights)
(Geneva: Pierre Cailler,
1956).

If you wish I'll give you
My morning, my morning gay
With all my light hair
                    That you love;
                    My green eyes
                    And golden
                    If you wish.
I'll give you all the sounds
                    That are made
            When the morning awakens
                    In the sun
            And the water that flows
            In the fountain
                    Close by;
And then again the evening that will come fast
            The evening of my soul so sad
                    It could cry
            And my hands so small
With my heart that must near yours
                    Be kept.

Le Tigre

Roi d'Espagne
  Prenez votre manteau
    Et un couteau
      Au jardin zoologique
        Il y a un tigre paralytique
       Mais royal
         Et le regarder fait mal.

■

Le Cheval

Cheval blessé meurt sans hennir
  Doux cheval
J'irai te voir mourir.

■

Le Zèbre

Ne crois pas Nicole
  Que le zèbre soit un animal
  Comme le cheval
Le zèbre est un danseur espagnol
  Dont je raffole.

The Tiger

King of Spain
    Take your mantle
        And a knife
           To the zoological garden
               There is a paralytic tiger
            But royal
               And looking at him makes one ill.

From *Le Carnet des nuits*.

■

The Horse

Wounded horse dies without a whinny
    Gentle horse
I shall go and see you die

■

The Zebra

Don't believe Nicole
    That the zebra is an animal
    Like the horse
The zebra is a Spanish dancer
    Whom I adore.

Marie Laurencin

In 'Hamac' Blaise Cendrars says to Apollinaire: 'Tu as longtemps écrit à l'ombre d'un tableau / A l'Arabesque tu songeais' (see above). The painting in question is very likely the one by Marie Laurencin that was hung in Apollinaire's apartment (see plate 9). Cendrars is suggesting that it was this painting that, like a Muse, inspired the poet as he sat writing. In the next line the 'Arabesque' is definitely an allusion to Marie Laurencin. Apollinaire often used the term as an epithet for his mistress. On one occasion he has Marie possessed by the 'demon of the arabesque.'

'Arabesque' becomes, then, the personification of a style full of rounded intertwinings, anything but a cubist style. As a kind of nickname for Marie Laurencin it takes on a rapid-fire sequence of associations: serpent, serpentine, dancer, Salome, Loie Fuller (a serpentine dancer of the day).

But how did Marie Laurencin come to be called a cubist painter, and by what right can one call her a poet?

Born in Paris in 1885, Marie Laurencin attended the École de Sèvres and the Académie Humbert. In 1906 she began exhibiting at the Salon des Indépendants, and in May of the following year, at the instigation of Picasso, she met Apollinaire in the shop of the art dealer Clovis Sagot.

Their liaison lasted about five years and was marked by a variety of artistic activity. In 1908 they posed together for the Douanier Rousseau's *Muse Inspiring the Poet*, and later in the year they attended the Rousseau banquet described by Gertrude Stein in *The Autobiography of Alice B. Toklas*.[1] It was thanks to Apollinaire that works by Marie Laurencin appeared in every cubist show in 1911 and 1912. Albert Gleizes, describing the Salon des Indépendants of 1911, writes: 'In Room 41 we—Le Fauconnier, Léger, Delaunay, Metzinger and myself—grouped ourselves, adding to our number at the request of Guillaume Apollinaire who was following the arrangements with the most lively interest, Marie Laurencin.'[2] In *Les Peintres cubistes* (1913) Apollinaire classifies her as a 'scientific cubist' and devotes a chapter to her work.[3]

Whatever terms one might use, then, to characterize her style, Marie Laurencin was indeed a cubist; and to ignore her presence in the movement is to blot out the all-important feminine element. But how does this make her a poet? The answer lies in part in a hoax perpetrated by Apollinaire in 1909. With the complicity of the editor of *Les Marges* (The margins), Eugène Montfort, and under the euphonious pseudonym Louise Lalanne, he wrote a series of critical essays on the women writers of the day—Colette, the Countess de Noailles, Gérard d'Houville, and others. The readers in time began asking that Louise Lalanne reveal her own talent as a poet. It was apparently at this point that Apollinaire called on Marie for help. She produced some verses in what she imagined to be the manner of Louise Lalanne. One of them, 'Le Présent,' is printed above. It

1. New York: Vintage, 1990. See pp. 103–7.

2. Edward F. Fry, *Cubism* (New York: McGraw Hill, 1966), 172.

3. *Oeuvres complètes de Guillaume Apollinaire*, ed. Michel Décaudin, vol. 4 (Paris: Balland et Lecat, 1966).

is not particularly original; after all, it is a pastiche. And it is not at all cubist. But it has the grace and charm that Apollinaire discerned in his mistress's paintings without the demonic undertone.

The second poem printed above is postcubist. It appeared in Picabia's dadaist magazine *391* in 1917. Like many dadaist texts, it combines typographical play with irrational or nonsensical imagery. There seems to be a mysterious tie between the paralytic tiger and the king of Spain. Are they both at once victim and executioner? In any case, Marie Laurencin is a long way here from Louise Lalanne; in fact she seems closest of all to Max Jacob.

Long after Apollinaire's death, Marie Laurencin gave this verse the title 'Le Tigre' and published it as the liminary piece along with a dozen other small poems ('Le Cheval,' 'Le Zèbre,' 'Les Oiseaux,' etc.) under the collective title *Petit Bestiaire* (Small bestiary) in *Le Carnet des nuits* (The notebook of the nights) in 1956. It is hardly fair to compare these pieces with the concise, pithy quatrains of Apollinaire's *Bestiaire,* but they do have the quality he prized above all others, the element of surprise.

HÉLÈNE D'OETTINGEN

12.

Kilima-N'Djaro

Le sinistre gronde.
Seul l'esprit voltige sous la giboulée de la tourmente.
Le refuge de voyageurs égarés . . .
Tremble le sommet de la montagne comme un peuplier abandonné.
Ce ne sont pas les Alpes ni les Pyrénées

Ces noms si doux!
De troupeaux de bergers
Parfois un guide avec un mort . . .

Ni guide ni pasteurs!

Une force inconnue m'appelle
Peut-être la voix de cette étoile perchée sur la dernière hauteur
Peut-être le désir de voir les espaces qui cachent l'Europe . . .

Quelle glace!
Ni profil ni face
La couleur s'est effondrée avant d'y parvenir
Mon haleine se change en un flot de sang caillé
Mes lèvres cessent de murmurer une prière
La nuit comble tout sans combler le vacarme
Ma montre chante comme une abeille enfermée dans un verre . . .

Si c'est la mort je prie celui qui me trouvera

Kilimanjaro

The volcano rumbles.
Alone the spirit flutters under the shower of the gale.
The refuge of lost travellers. . . .
The summit of the mountain trembles like a forsaken poplar.
It is not the Alps or the Pyrenees

Those names so gentle!
Of flocks of shepherds
At times a guide with a dead body. . . .

Neither guide nor shepherds!

An unknown force is calling me
Perhaps the voice of that star perched on the last height
Perhaps the desire to see the spaces that conceal Europe. . . .

What a mirror!
Neither profile nor face
The color caved in before reaching it
My breath is changing into a flood of curdled blood
My lips stop murmuring a prayer
Night fills all without filling the din
My watch sings like a bee shut up in a glass. . . .

If it is to be death I beg the one who finds me

From
Hélène d'Oettingen
[Léonard Pieux, pseud.],
in *Nord-Sud*, no. 3 (May
1917), 10–11.

D'emporter mon passeport et cette photographie
Et cette mèche de cheveux qui me réchauffe de son dernier effort
D'adresser tout cela au 229 du Boulevard Raspail à Paris.

■

Clameurs

Cette apothéose m'accable
Jamais ce mot ne fut moins approprié au bonheur
Suis-je gardien des étoiles au bord d'un affreux danger
Berger imaginaire perdu dans une vaste forêt
Les Dieux sont en marbre
Au fond d'un musée
Un monstre quadrupède me fait signe d'approcher
Un ver solitaire quitte le vieux bocal
L'air est bleu les voiles frémissent
Et la mer glorieuse misérable Tantale
T'invite au voyage . . .
Un bouquet jaune comme un remords
Blesse ma vue
La cage
La roue
L'infect ennui de l'humanité entière
Et personne personne pour briser mes fers!

To take my passport and the photograph
And this lock of hair which makes its final effort to warm me
To address all that to 229 Boulevard Raspail in Paris.

■

Outcries

This apotheosis crushes me
Never was this word less related to happiness
Am I the guardian of the stars on the edge of a frightful danger
Imaginary shepherd lost in a vast forest
The gods are made of marble
Deep inside a museum
A quadruped monster beckons me to approach
A tapeworm comes out of the old jar
The air is blue the sails quiver
And the glorious sea wretched Tantalus
Invites you on a voyage . . .
A bouquet yellow like remorse
Hurts my view
The cage
The wheel
The vile ennui of all mankind
And no one no one to break my chains!

Pieux [pseud.], from *Nord-Sud*, no. 10 (December 1917), 7.

**[A
Il y a]**

Déjà ta jeunesse fleurie s'évapore doucement
'Il y a' ton nom évoque le tout existant sur la terre
Etat compacte du volatile
Surface lisse ou criblée de pleurs
Il y a aussi le trajet jusqu'au grand but que tu ignores
Il y a des yeux bleus ou noirs de femmes
Que tu suivras toujours
Comme un chiffonnier qui suit la lueur fugace d'un bec de gaz
Comme un scaphandrier qui suit la lueur des étoiles
Que réflète la surface houleuse de la mer
Comme moi qui cherche à tracer l'ombre de mon amour
Sur le coeur même de la terre.

[To
Il y a]

Already your flowering youth is gently evaporating
Il y a—there is—your name evokes the all that exists on the earth
Compact state of the volatile
Surface glossy or riddled with tears
Il y a—there is—also the trip to the great goal unknown by you
Il y a—there are—women's blue or black eyes
That you will always pursue
Like a ragman who follows the fleeting glimmer of a gas lamp
Like a diver who follows the glimmer of the stars
That is reflected by the swelling surface of the sea
Like myself as I try to trace the shadow of my love
On the very heart of the earth

Printed under the pseudonym Léonard Pieux in the catalog for the exhibition of Iliazd-Picasso at the Musée National des Arts Moderne Pompidou, Paris, 1978.

Hélène d'Oettingen

One of the main headquarters on Montparnasse during the struggle for cubism was 229 Boulevard Raspail, home of the Baroness Hélène d'Oettingen and her brother, the painter Serge Jastredzoff Férat.

The Baroness has often been described as an eccentric; Gertrude Stein called her 'not uninteresting.' Max Jacob is one of the few to give a detailed description of the Baroness in her home. Here is an excerpt: 'On important occasions one would go up in the morning on the brand new elevator to the modern-style seventh floor of 229 Boulevard Raspail. From the height of her high heels which lengthened her lengthy graciousness, she would greet you with unsubdued compassion, still walking to and fro in the panelled green house next to the studio with her arms crossed on a pair of yellow moiré pajamas.'[1]

For Jacob everything about the Baroness was profusion and largesse. From tea she would always save the roast beef sandwiches for the more poverty-stricken artists, such as Modigliani, Survage, Ortiz, and Jacob himself. She gave Russian lessons to Picasso at the time he was courting Olga. Above all, it was this generosity that allowed Apollinaire to revitalize *Les Soirées de Paris*. Under the name Jean Cérusse (read *C'est russe*, It is Russian) the Baroness and her brother managed the affairs of the

1. Neal Oxenhandler, *Max Jacob and 'Les Feux de Paris,'* trans. L. C. Breunig, University of California Publications in Modern Philology 35, no. 4 (Berkeley and Los Angeles: University of California Press, 1964), 299.

review and kept it afloat financially until the First World War forced it to close down.

She was a prolific writer, one of the few to contribute to both *SIC* and *Nord-Sud,* as well as to *Les Soirées.* She wrote novels and prose essays under the pseudonym Roch Grey and poetry under the name Léonard Pieux, and she painted under the name François Angiboult.

The Baroness and her brother were among the first to recognize Douanier Rousseau. Among the paintings they bought is the large self-portrait that hangs above portraits of the Baroness, Picasso, Serge Férat, and Léopold Survage in a sketch by De Chirico (see plate 10).

The lyric poetry has certain cubist traits. 'Kilima-N'Djaro' seeks to maintain an exclamatory tone so as to heighten the contrast with the prosaic conclusion, which contains the references to the passport photograph and the Paris address. As a piece of literary collage this conclusion reminds one of the 'for sale' sign at the end of Max Jacob's 'Invitation au voyage' (see above).

In 'Clameurs' (see above) the line fragments convey an overall sense of oppression not unlike certain evocations in Reverdy and Huidobro, except that the latter are considerably more restrained, and their vocabularies tend to be more generic.

Still under the name Léonard Pieux, the Baroness collaborated with the cubist painter Léopold Survage to produce on his woodcuts, thirteen of them, a series of handwritten verses beginning on the title page with the words: 'Accordez-moi une audience Et je vous réciterai les vers d'un

Plate 10. *The Baroness d'Oettingen with friends,* pencil sketch by Giorgio de Chirico. Published by permission of VAGA (Visual Artists and Galleries Association).

poète inconnu . . . ' (Grant me an audience and I shall recite to you the verses of an unknown poet . . .). In the illustration, against a background of rectangular buildings—a favorite motif of Survage's—with their windows and curtains and silhouettes of pedestrians forming a mysterious cityscape (see plate 11), the following lines of verse are scattered among the roofs and walls:

Plate 11. *L'homme glisse . . .*, woodcut illustration by Léopold Survage for poem by the Baroness d'Oettingen (Léonard Pieux, pseud.). Courtesy of Mr. Carl Little, New York, N.Y.

> L'homme glisse le long des maisons figées stoïquement
> Perpendiculaire
> comme elles
> Mouvant ornement
> Fiction ardente
> Sa fragilité contredit la durée de ses tourments

> (The man slips along the stoically congealed houses
> Perpendicular
> like them
> A moving ornament
> Burning fiction
> His fragility contradicts the duration of his torments)

Particularly striking is the tall perpendicular word *perpendiculaire*, which imitates its meaning in much the same way as Mallarmé's line in 'L'Après-midi d'un faune' (The afternoon of a faun): 'Une sonore, vaine et monotone ligne' (A sonorous, vain and monotonous line). The reference on the title page to an 'unknown' poet remains ambiguous. It could simply be

the Baroness herself as Léonard Pieux, or a mythical poet, an Orpheus, or a poet 'of the unknown' like Rimbaud. In any case, poet and painter become almost one in this work thanks to the tight connection between verses and woodcuts. Some of the same motifs are repeated in Survage's 1917 portrait of the Baroness (see plate 12).

The Baroness's love of word and name play is responsible for a short postcubist poem addressed to the Russian artist and impresario Ilya Zdanevitch, better known as Iliazd, in 1924 (see above). The Baroness must have had in mind the poems of both Rimbaud and Apollinaire where each line begins with the statement 'Il y a' (There is, there are) as if to call a thing into being by naming it, thus evoking, as Léonard Pieux writes in line 2, 'le tout existant sur la terre' and at the same time keeping the intimacy of the four letters of a beloved proper name.

After the Baroness's death in 1950 Iliazd persuaded Picasso to illustrate one of the novels (or 'epics,' as she preferred to call them) entitled *Chevaux de minuit* (Midnight horses), which she had written under the name Roch Grey.[2] Unfortunately, profusion becomes prolixity in this 'dishevelled' work, as one critic called it; but without it we would not have the gracious horses of the 'equestrian ballet' of Picasso's bestiary.

Plate 12. *Baroness d'Oettingen*, portrait by Léopold Survage. Copyright 1991, ARS, N.Y./ADAGP.

2. *Chevaux de Minuit* was printed in triptych by Degré 41, Cannes and Paris, in 1949. In 1956 fifty-two copies were published under the name Iliazd. The epic was reproduced in the catalog of the Iliazd-Picasso exhibition at the Musée d'Art Moderne de la Ville de Paris in 1976.

RAYMOND RADIGUET

13.

Poème

un édredon rouge   à   la fenêtre
des fleurs dans l'entrejambe   du   ca-
leçon   ce jardin tiède dans la giroflée
parfum de linge tiède séché
le marronnier chante
serait-ce   ces bougies roses irrégulièrement plantées
ou bien   un   oiseau
su   la co d   le li g   d n   e
   r   r e   n   e   a   s
   e   i   a ch   e q   m
ch m se m n   ott   ui   e
       t   d l s br
      en   e   as

Poem

a red eiderdown   at   the window
flowers in the inner lining   of the   draw-
ers   this tepid gilly-flower garden
aroma of dried tepid linen
the chestnut-tree is singing
could it be   those pink candles irregularly planted
or else   a   bird
o   the li   the li   e   d   n es
  n   ne   n n   a c
s i t wi   ou   sl   ve wh ch h lds
  h r   th   t   ee   i   o
o t he   rms t   m
  u   r a   o   e

Signed Raimon Rajky, from *SIC,* no. 30 (June 1918), 103. See also David Noakes, *Raymond Radiguet,* Collection Poètes d'aujourd'hui (Paris: Seghers, 1968).

Poème

Ligne d'horizon

Morceaux de tête

Dans le rocking chair

Murs

L'éphéméride est déjà à après demain

Un camion automobile écrase nos ombres

S.V.P.

On se bouscule aux portes du ciel ou des Grands magazins

Les paroles se cognent

Articles pour voyage mais

Il y a plus de monde au rayon des ustensiles de cuisine   l'é-

Charpe des maires

Au bout des rails

La   mer

Poem

Horizon line

Pieces of head

In the rocking chair

Walls

The ephemeris is already up to day-after-tomorrow

A motor truck is crushing our shadows

S.V.P.

People are jostling at the gates of heaven or Department stores

Words are bumping into each other

Tourists' commodities but

There are more people at the kitchen utensil counter   th-

e Sash of the mayors

At the end of the rails

The   sea

From *SIC*, no. 33 (November 1918), 140. See also Noakes, *Radiguet*.

Plan

Combien êtes-vous?
je ne sais compter que jusqu'à onze
parlez plus fort je ne vous entends plus
je ne vois que quelques chaises
et la lampe

LA VILLE

un seul fleuve
le trait bleu indique le fleuve

Ne t'en va pas déjà
Les rues se cherchent
se rencontrent
A la ligne.
Lignes fuyantes.
Ils s'en vont
Tous dans une direction différente

LE PASSÉ

ce qui s'est passé il y a
mille ans
non
il y a trois minutes

Map

How many of you are there?
I can't count beyond eleven
speak louder I don't hear you any more
I can only see some chairs
       and the lamps
          THE CITY
     a single river
     the blue stroke indicates the river
Don't go away yet
The streets search and meet
      each other
On a new line
Fleeting lines.
      The people go away
Each in a different direction
       THE PAST
     what happened a thousand
          years ago
   no
     three minutes ago

From *SIC*, nos. 40–41
(February 1919), 106–7.
See also Noakes,
Radiguet.

Cadran sans Aiguilles

Les heures qui nous regardaient :
Ascenseurs s'envolent de leurs cages lourds de prières
                    Complet
Sur le paillasson restent les dernières

                              Des fenêtres s'éveillent les étoiles
                              ont sommeil
                              Partie de l'autre côté des Océans
                              L'aube arrive dans ma chambre

Un placard
Il y fait nuit même pendant le jour
Les journées de la semaine prochaine attendent.

Handless Clock

The hours that kept looking at us:
Elevators fly out of their cages heavy with prayers
           Full
The last ones stay on the doormat

           Windows awaken stars
           are sleepy
           Leaving the other side of the Oceans
           Dawn arrives in my bedroom

A cupboard
It is night time there even during the day
The days of the next week stand by

From *SIC*, nos. 40–41 (March 1919), 107. See also Noakes, *Radiguet*.

Raymond Radiguet

André Salmon relates that when Raymond Radiguet, at the age of fifteen, presented Apollinaire with some verses that showed the influence of *Alcools*, Apollinaire, assuming that he was the victim of a hoax, flew into a rage. Upon learning the truth, he simply said bitingly, 'Don't give up, Monsieur, Arthur Rimbaud didn't write his masterpiece until he was seventeen.'

Radiguet was indeed the child prodigy of cubism. Born near Paris, at Parc St. Maur, in 1903, he was discovered by Salmon, who was a friend of his father's. He quickly came to know Albert-Birot and the team of *SIC*, and in June 1918 he published his first poem, a cubist piece for *SIC* called 'Poème' and signed Raimon Rajky. Others followed (with the correct signature, upon Salmon's advice), but by 1919 Radiguet was already turning away from the cubist phase. He had only four more years to live, fruitful years that saw the writing of the two prose fiction masterpieces, *Le Diable au corps* (The devil in the flesh) and *Le Bal du comte d'Orgel* (The ball of the count d'Orgel), and the publication by Kahnweiler of the satire *Les Pélican*, with etchings by Henri Laurens, in 1921. Kahnweiler also published posthumously (1926) Radiguet's *Denise* with lithographs by Juan Gris.

The four poems above first appeared in *SIC*. 'Plan' (Map) is printed in its definitive version from *Le Bonnet d'âne* (Donkey's bonnet).[1] The opening line of the first 'Poème' above, 'un édredon rouge à la fenêtre,' is undoubtedly a borrowing from Apollinaire's 'Zone': 'Une famille transporte un édredon rouge / comme vous transportez votre coeur.' And this may well be the line that so angered the older poet. It does not necessarily follow, however, that Radiguet was a plagiarist or a parodist. With this fragment as a kind of collage, he could simply be rendering homage to Apollinaire in much the same way that Cendrars does in 'Hamac' or Juan Gris does in *La Montre*.

It is in the conclusion of 'Poème' that one is particularly inclined to detect the hand of Apollinaire. The scattered letters, which, if one puts them back in their natural order, spell out the words

> sur la corde le linge danse
> chemise manchotte qui me
> tend les bras

are, in their jumbled order, the representation of precisely that: linen dancing on the line, a sleeveless shirt extending its arms to me. Apollinaire had used scattered letters in 'Voyage' (in *Calligrammes*) to designate somewhat more obviously the stars and the moon in a cloudless sky. This calligram had appeared in *Les Soirées de Paris* in 1914.

In the next poem above, also titled 'Poème' the opening line, 'Ligne d'horizon,' not only designates itself as a horizontal line but sets the top

1. See David Noakes, *Raymond Radiguet*, Collection Poètes d'aujourd'hui (Paris: Seghers, 1968).

part of a frame of which 'Au bout des rails' would be the bottom, opening into the sea. One cannot help recalling Huidobro's *Horizon carré* and the importance both poets attached to the representation of lines. Within the framework of 'Poème,' among the heterogeneous items named one finds a line set off from the others, a single clause: 'Les paroles se cognent.' Is not this an accurate statement of the author's view of the action within his own poem?

In 'Plan' Radiguet develops the linear theme, enumerating types of lines in the middle section in much the same way that Apollinaire lists cords in 'Liens' (*Calligrammes*). The lines become fleeting (*fuyantes*), and unknown beings (human beings, we can only assume, there being no masculine plural antecedent for *Ils*) all go away in different directions. This radiation in space suggests a similar temporal radiation, as the poet evokes the mysterious elasticity of time past.

In the fourth poem, 'Cadran sans aiguilles,' time is jumbled, both by direct statement and by allusion. The everyday objects of the household mix with the handless clock of the title to call up a topsy-turvy world in time.

PIERRE REVERDY

14.

Route

Sur le seuil personne
   Ou ton ombre
Un souvenir qui resterait
La route passe
   Et les arbres parlent plus près
Qu'y a-t-il derrière
    Un mur
      des voix
Les nuages qui s'élevèrent
Au moment où je passais là
Et tout le long une barrière
    Où sont ceux qui n'entreront pas

Road

On the threshold no one
        Or your shadow
A memory that would remain
The road goes by
      And the trees speak more closely
What is there behind
        A wall
          voices
The clouds that rose
The moment I went by
And all along the fence
      Where those are who will not enter

From *Les Ardoises du toit* (Roof slates) (1918), in *Poésies* (Paris: Flammarion, 1969), 176.

Sur le Seuil

Dans le coin où elle s'est blottie
Tristesse ou vide
Le vent tourne
On entend un cri
Personne n'a voulu se plaindre
Mais la lampe vient de s'éteindre
Et passe sans faire de bruit
Une main tiède
Sur tes paupières
Où pèse la journée finie
Tout se dresse
Et dans le monde qui se presse
Les objets mêlés à la nuit
La forme que j'avais choisie
Si la lumière
Revivait comme on se réveille
Il resterait dans mon oreille
La voix joyeuse qui la veille
En rentrant m'avait poursuivi

On the Threshold

In the corner where she crouched
                    Sadness or void
The wind turns
                    A cry is heard
No one wanted to complain
But the lamp has just gone out
                    And passes without a noise
A warm hand
                    On your eyelids
                    Where the day's end weighs down
Everything stands erect
                    And in the world that hurries along
The objects mingled with the night
                    The form that I had chosen
If the light
                    Lived again as one wakes up
There would remain in my ear
The joyful voice that the evening before
Had pursued me on my way home

From *Les Ardoises du toit*,
in *Poésies*, 177.

Départ

L'horizon s'incline
                 Les jours sont plus longs
                 Voyage
       Un coeur saute dans une cage
                 Un oiseau chante
                 Il va mourir
   Une autre porte va s'ouvrir
              Au fond du couloir
                 Où s'allume
                 Une étoile
 Une femme brune
         La lanterne du train qui part

Departure

The horizon slopes away
                    The days are longer
                    Trip
          A heart hops in a cage
                    A bird sings
                    It is going to die
Another door is going to open
               At the end of the corridor
                    Where a star
                    Begins to shine
A dark-haired woman
               The lantern of the departing train

From *Les Ardoises du toit,*
in *Poésies,* 179.

Air

Oubli

porte fermée

Sur la terre inclinée

Un arbre tremble

Et seul

Un oiseau chante

Sur le toit

Il n'y a plus de lumière

Que le soleil

Et les signes que font tes doigts

Air

Forgetting
closed door
On the slanting earth
A tree trembles
And alone
A bird sings

On the roof
There is no longer any light
But the sun

And the signs made by your fingers

From *Les Ardoises du toit*,
in *Poésies*, 186.

Poste

Pas une tête ne dépasse
                              Un doigt se lève
Puis c'est la voix que l'on connait
        Un signal
                                une note brève
        Un homme part
Là-haut un nuage qui passe
                Personne ne rentre
Et la nuit garde son secret

Post

Not a head stands out
                    A finger rises
Then it is the voice that one knows
        A signal
                        a brief note
        A man leaves
Up above a cloud that passes by
            No one goes in
And the night keeps its secret

From *Les Ardoises du toit*,
in *Poésies*, 187.

Adieu

La lueur plus loin que la tête
Le saut du coeur
Sur la pente où l'air roule sa voix
les rayons de la roue
le soleil dans l'ornière

Au carrefour
près du talus
une prière
Quelques mots que l'on n'entend pas
Plus près du ciel
Et sur ses pas
le dernier carré de lumière

Adieu

The glimmer farther away than the head

The heart-skip

On the slope where the air rolls its voice

The spokes of the wheel

the sun in the rut

At the crossroads

near the embankment

a prayer

Some words that are not heard

Nearer the sky

And on its steps

the last square of light

From *Cravates de chanvre* (Neckties of hemp) (1922) in *Plupart du temps* (Paris: Flammarion, 1967), 370.

Pierre Reverdy Ⓜ

Pierre Reverdy is generally considered the cubist poet par excellence, although he himself rejected the term. D. H. Kahnweiler sets him alongside Juan Gris, calling them the 'pure' artists of the group. Reverdy is also looked upon as the most articulate aesthetician among the poets.

Born in 1889 in Narbonne, in southern France, he moved to Paris at the age of twenty-one and made his way to the Bateau-Lavoir, on Montmartre. He worked for a while, appropriately enough, as a typesetter. His first publication was a collection of prose poems in the manner of Max Jacob (1915). In 1917 he launched with Paul Dermée the periodical that came to be looked upon as the official organ of cubism, *Nord-Sud*, named for the Métro line that connects Montmartre, in the north, with Montparnasse, in the south. After *La Lucarne oval* (Oval skylight), whose title so antagonized Huidobro, Reverdy published the volume of poetry that is usually hailed as his best, *Les Ardoises du toit* (Roof slates), in 1918.

The poems reproduced above are fairly typical of Reverdy's style, especially during the cubist period, and one can deduce certain characteristics that apply generally. They are short. Reverdy's poems rarely take up more than a single page. The title is usually one word, an abstraction more likely than not, and one it is up to the reader to connect with the text. The verses are for the most part 'line-fragments,'[1] incomplete sen-

1. Robert W. Greene, 'Pierre Reverdy,' *Six French Poets of Our Time* (Princeton: Princeton University Press, 1979).

tences, ellipses, single words, brief notations. 'Je ne pense pas; je note' (I do not think; I note), wrote Reverdy in an echo of Descartes's *Cogito*. Each poem has a different typographical arrangement. There is rarely a stable lefthand margin. Some lines begin in the middle or on the right, with or without an uppercase initial letter. The absence of punctuation and conjunctions heightens the ambiguity of the line-to-line relationship. The alternating printed characters and blanks on the page create shaped poems, which Reverdy termed 'la poésie plastique' (plastic poetry). The viewer is expected to become both reader and spectator, admiring the appearance of the ensemble as he would a painting by Gris. For the poems are self-sufficient objects, 'cristaux déposés après l'effervescent contact de l'esprit avec la réalité' (crystals deposited after the effervescent contact of the spirit with reality).

If Reverdy partakes of cubist theory in the notion of the poem as object, his tendency to conceptualize the elements of reality, substituting the generic for the particular, is also typical of cubism. In this respect he carries on the French classical tradition, which, with Racine and Mallarmé, preferred the word *fleur* to any one of the five hundred–odd flowers and plants that fill the works of Shakespeare. Let the other cubists sing of the Eiffel Tower, of Panhards, or red eiderdowns. Reverdy will not particularize he will simply note:

Un mur	('Route')
On entend un cri	('Sur le seuil')

Un oiseau chante	('Départ' and 'Air')
Un homme part	('Poste')

Reverdy thus achieves a simplicity and a purity of expression that distinguishes him from the other cubists. Among the surrealists Paul Eluard alone will vie with him in this respect.

But what do these 'crystals' communicate? Here is where each reader steps in to do his own decoding. Take 'Route,' for example. On a second or third (or fourth) reading one senses a connection between the negation of the opening line, 'Sur le seuil personne,' and that of the final line, 'Où sont ceux qui n'entreront pas,' these two being in fact the only negatives of the poem. The threshold of the first line apparently remains vacant up to the end of the poem, if we are to believe the reference in the last line to those who will not enter. But does the negation not presuppose the presence of those who *will* cross over? This implicit affirmation assures the actuality of a *terra incognita* that is hinted at by the various line fragments. And even though the last two lines of the poem conjure up a depressing image of those standing along the 'barrière' (meaning both 'fence' and 'barrier'), who will never cross over the threshold, we are left with a confident belief in the reality of this unnamed land.

One is tempted in reading Reverdy to supply literary parallels and precursors. Are those in 'Route' who 'will not enter' not the damned of Dante's Inferno? And is it not through the *seuil* that one crosses over to Paradiso? The trees that talk in line five allude perhaps to Homer's oaks of Dodona, with their whispering leaves. And so forth. But comparisons of this kind do Reverdy an injustice by ignoring his preference for the generic. If he makes no effort to individualize a word like *seuil*, it is obviously because he wants the reader to see it as an abstraction, as part of a dialectic. He thus seeks to universalize his own contradictory feelings, as we noted in 'Route,' where belief and nonbelief, hope and depression, struggle. Underlying such oppositions is a pervasive malaise deriving from a complex of causes, but above all, perhaps, from one's sense of foreignness in a hostile world.

The simplicity of a Reverdy poem can be quite deceptive. The everyday vocabulary, the simple syntax, the correctness of the line fragments, the preponderance of generic terms, the unity of style, at once hide and reveal the poetic spark that is the raison d'être of the poem.

ANDRÉ SALMON

15.

Prikaz

Innocence du monde

Quand l'arbre de science avec sa pomme ronde

Est un arbre de mai

L'Arbre de la Liberté

Adoré

Insulté

Planté

Devant la cathédrale vide de chantres

Quand de la nudité d'Eve seul resplendit le ventre.

Quand Adam adamite a vendu ses habits

Pour être Adam

Où bien, en a vêtu le déserteur

Tel qu'on voit son maître vêtir le serviteur,

Quand l'Eve est une grande dame

Déshabillée par les soldats ivres, la farce ayant sa place au plus fort du
   drame.

Innocence du monde

Lorsque la pomme ronde

Crépite

Mélinite, cheddite, dynamite, ypérite,

Quand le serpent à tête plate

Collant ses écailles noires au fût du bel arbre écarlate,

Aux yeux du plus pauvre d'esprit n'est absolument rien

Prikaz

Innocence of the world.
When the tree of knowledge with its round apple
Is a May tree
The Tree of Liberty
Adored
Insulted
Planted
In front of the cathedral emptied of cantors
When of Eve's nakedness the belly alone is resplendent.
When Adam the Adamite sold his clothes
To become Adam
Or rather clothed the deserter
Just as one sees the servant dressed by his master.
When Eve is a grande dame
Stripped by drunken soldiers, since farce has its place in the
        drama.
Innocence of the world
When the round apple
Crepitates
Melinites, cheddites, dynamites, yperites,
When the flat-headed serpent
Sticking his black scales to the shaft of the handsome, scarlet tree
In the eyes of the poorest in spirit is absolutely nothing

From
Carreaux (Tiles) (Paris:
Gallimard, 1918), 9–11.

Qu'une enseigne de pharmacien
Ou bien le signe gravé sur les boutons d'uniforme
Des médecins militaires gantés de caoutchouc
Traînant dans les salons un relent d'iodoforme,
Quand ils vont faire l'amour sous prétexte de thé
Avec la soeur laïque épuisée de bonté
D'extase et de dégoût.
Innocence du monde
A la clarté dansante
Des flammes qu'alimentent
Le bitume et les jus du maître d'Amsterdam
L'Ermitage est en feu, le Musée d'Alexandre
Réchauffe son deuil à ses cendres
Et l'étudiant aux trop longs cheveux
Coiffé d'une casquette verte à turban bleu,
Tout à la fois soldat, juge, consul et bourreau
A la langue ardente offre encore la librairie de Diderot.
Le plomb des imprimeries s'écoule ainsi qu'un fleuve
Pour fondre l'alphabet des humanités neuves
Et dans un galetas du quartier Kameny
Par un père mourant deux fiancés sont bénis.
Les ombres de ce qui meurt composent sur les murs rougis à blanc une
　　ronde.
Une ronde de naissances.

But a pharmacist's insignia
Or else the sign marked on the uniform buttons
Of rubber-gloved military doctors
Trailing into the parlors a whiff of iodoform,
When under the pretext of a cup of tea they go to make love
With the secular nurse who is worn out from goodness
Ecstasy and disgust.
Innocence of the world
In the dancing light
Of the flames that feed on
The tar and the juices of the master of Amsterdam
The Hermitage is on fire, the Alexander Museum
From its ashes reheats its mourning
And the student with overly long hair
Wearing a green hat topped by a blue turban,
Soldier, judge, consul and executioner all together
To the burning tongue offers again the library of Diderot.
The lead of the printing presses flows like a river
To melt the alphabet of the new humanities
And in a hovel of the Kameny section
By a dying father two fiancés are blessed.
The shadows of that which dies compose on the reddened wall bled
        white a round
A round of births.

Innocence du monde,
Innocence! Innocence!

Voix d'un professeur en chaire à l'Université
Au delà de la Bourse et du port, sur l'autre rive :
        'Aucun auteur ne peut citer
          Aucun cas constaté de démence collective'.
Voix d'un Cosaque du Kouban tourné du côté de la Mecque:
        'Ce qui est écrit arrive'.

Un conseil de soldats se tient à l'Opéra.
Une corneille grise et noire poursuivie par les rats
Traverse la Néva plantée de réverbères inclinés, car la débâcle
    commence.
Innocence!
Innocence!...

Innocence of the world,
Innocence! Innocence!

Voice of a University professor
Beyond the stock exchange and the port, on the other bank:
       'No writer can cite
         A single verified case of collective madness.'
Voice of a Cossack of Kuban turning towards Mecca:
       'That which is written comes to pass.'

A consultation of soldiers is held at the Opera.
A gray and black crow pursued by the rats
Crosses the Neva which is planted with tilting lamps, for the debacle has
    begun.
Innocence!
Innocence! ...

Peindre

Je compare au vol terrible de Nungesser l'oeuvre illimité de
    Picasso
Et j'aperçois une promesse d'infini
Dans ce bouquet ovale et calculé de Severini.
Baudelaire romantique encore tremble et s'effare
Quoiqu'il ne fût jamais si pur que dans ses Phares.
Je voudrais qu'on pût dire, ô ciels mirés dans l'eau,
Riches jardins du ciel où cueillir tout l'été,
Dire avec le ton des bonnes gens entêtés :
Il fait un temps de Tiepolo!
Et pourquoi ne pas soupirer, Madame!
J'ai du Whistler à l'âme!

Trois pommes de Cézanne
    La guitare de Pablo
Font dans le jour qui se fane
    Un profond tableau,
Je suis hanté par les images!
    Captif d'un monde récréé

Mon pays n'est qu'un paysage
    En son cadre doré

Painting

I compare the awesome flight of Nungesser to the limitless work of
    Picasso

Excerpts from *Carreaux*,
79, 84, 97–98, 105–7.

And I perceive a promise of the infinite

In that regulated oval bouquet of Severini.

Baudelaire the Romantic still quakes and shudders

Although he was never so pure as in his 'Beacons.'

I wish one could say, oh heavens mirrored in the water,

Rich gardens of the sky where an entire summer can be gathered,

Say with the tone of good resolute people:

'What Tiepolo weather today!'

And why not sigh, Madame!

I've got Whistler in my soul!

Three apples of Cézanne
    The guitar of Pablo

Make in the day that wanes
    A deep painting,

I am haunted by the images!
    Captive of a recreated world

My land is only a landscape
    In its gilded frame.

Par de très longs couloirs de toile peinte
    Mon âme à l'abandon
A la fille nue, à la sainte
    Réclame son pardon

Trois pommes de Cézanne
    La guitare de Pablo . . .

    ❖

Le peintre est mort.

La couleur a perdu son maître
Et la lumière son époux ;
Tant de formes qui pouvaient naître!
Tant de puits de clarté s'abîmant aux égouts!

Le peintre est mort.

Comme une lyre aux griffes des Ménades
La palette désaccordée
Se rompt dans un fracas de tilleul foudroyé
Dans un tumulte d'odeur, et la bête malade,
L'animal familier de l'artiste vaincu,
Le chat divin aux yeux de jour diffus,
Blessé par la lumière échappée au génie
    —Serve en sa gloire, absurde dans sa tyrannie—
La bête aux mouvements profonds et contenus,

Down the long print-lined corridors
    My forsaken soul
To the naked girl, to the woman saint
    Calls for its pardon.

Three apples of Cézanne
The guitar of Pablo . . .

The painter is dead

Color has lost its master
And light its spouse;
So many forms that could have been born!
So many wells of brightness sinking into the sewers!

The painter is dead.

Like a lyre with the claws of the Maenads
The palette that's out of tune
Breaks up with the crash of lightning-blasted linden,
In a tumult of odor, and the sick beast,
The pet of the artist who has succumbed,
The divine cat with daylight eyes diffused,
Wounded by the light that's escaped from the genius
    —A vassal in her glory, absurd in her tyranny—
The beast with deep, contained movements,

Maudissant la lumière insipide, importune,
Hurle au soleil ainsi qu'une chienne à la lune.

Le peintre est mort.

Le plancher geint sous le faix des espaces
Et sur le chevalet un profil qui s'efface . . .

❖

O place Clichy
O square d'Anvers
Jeux réfléchis
Du monde à l'envers.
O notre jeunesse
Gageures tenues
Et paris gagnés
Nos heures perdues
O jeunes années!

On faisait un choeur solide
Pour pavoiser la nuit vide
Des airs de notre façon :

Besnard
Binnard
Vuillard
Vollard

Cursing the insipid, importunate light,
Howls at the sun like a bitch at the moon.

The painter is dead.

The floor groans under the burden of the spaces
And on the easel a profile that is effaced . . .

❖

                    Oh place Clichy
                    Oh square d'Anvers
                         Resounding games
                    Of a topsy-turvy world
                      Oh our youthfulness
                    Wagers kept
                         And bets won
                    Our hours lost
                         Oh youthful years

We made a solid chorus
To ship-dress the empty night
With tunes of our making:

                    Besnard
                    Bonnard
                    Vuillard
                    Vollard

Apollinaire riait dans le creux de sa main,
Kees venu d'Amsterdam pour regarder les filles
Leur prenait du plaisir en prenant sa leçon
Linge, satin et chair qui brille.
Derain qui savait toutes choses
Et Picasso s'émerveillant
Époque bleue
Époque rose!
Le ciel frappé des signes d'un décret impérieux
Le ciel où tu lisais, Jacob, comme dans un roman
Le ciel tableau des poids et des mesures
Le ciel enseigne de celui qui nous faisait l'usure
Le ciel marin et ses tempêtes
Où le peintre gréait le vaisseau du poète
Où tant de nefs sombrées, nommées, ressuscitaient,
    et tous ces chiffres.
—Trésor réel, notre seul bien—
Que nous comptions sur cette mer de Chypre,
              Cyprien!

Apollinaire riait dans le creux de sa main,
Picasso couronnait un enfant merveilleux,
Le plus las s'appuyait sur le bras de Derain
Et Marie Laurencin en robe de mésange
       —Diane et Geneviève de Brabant—

Apollinaire would laugh in the hollow of his hand,
Kees down from Amsterdam to look over the girls
Took their pleasure with his own
Linen, satin and flesh that shines.
Derain who knew all things
And Picasso was filled with wonder
Blue period
Pink period!
The sky struck with the signs of an imperious decree
The sky where you read, Jacob, as in a novel
The sky table of weights and measures
The sky sign of our moneylender
The sky of the sea and the tempests
Where the painter rigged the vessel of the poet
Where so many ships, called by name would resuscitate,
     and all those figures.
—A real treasure, our only asset—
How we counted on that Cyprian Sea,
                    Cyprian!

Apollinaire would laugh in the hollow of his hand,
Picasso would crown a child of wonder,
The one who was most tired would lean on Derain's arm
And Marie Laurencin in a titmouse dress
          —Diane and Geneviève de Brabant—

D'une chanson rouvrait les yeux des anges
Et du couple perdu endormi sur un banc.
Dieu n'existe qu'on ne l'adore
Le temps n'est rien que l'on n'a point rêvé
Combien d'aurores
Avons-nous fait lever?

O mondes élargis de nos sages ivresses
O patries tirées du néant
O rue des Abbesses
O rue Ravignan!

With a song would open up the eyes of the angels
And of the lost couple sleeping on a bench.
God exists only if adored
Time is nothing if one has not dreamed
    How many dawns
    Have we got out of bed?

Oh worlds widened by our far-sighted intoxications
    Oh motherlands drawn from nowhere
     Oh rue des Abbesses
    Oh rue Ravignan!

André Salmon

One of the more successful etchings in Louis Marcoussis's series illustrating poems from Apollinaire's *Alcools* is the 'Poème lu au mariage d'André Salmon' (Poem read at the wedding of André Salmon). The poem itself was composed by Apollinaire in 1909 to celebrate the marriage, which took place on the eve of Bastille Day. The tricolor flags and bunting are flying, not for the Quatorze Juillet (July 14), 'but for my good friend André Salmon on his wedding day.'

The main components of Marcoussis's cubist still life (see plate 14) are connected with the inside of a bar, which is understandable enough when one reads in the poem how the two youths met. It was in 1903 in a 'caveau maudit' (wretched little dive), actually a not so sordid café on the Place Saint-Michel, where the poets would recite from their latest symbolist verses.

Born in Paris in 1881, Salmon, like Apollinaire, wanted to create a new poetic language, and the two of them with Max Jacob formed the nucleus around Picasso. It was in fact Salmon who named the Bateau-Lavoir the 'Rendez-vous des Poètes.' Salmon had a talent for names and was responsible for, among other titles, *Les Demoiselles d'Avignon*.

Like Apollinaire, Salmon passed through an elegiac phase comparable

to Picasso's blue and pink periods. His volumes *Poèmes* (1905) and *Les Féeries* (1907) prompted an appreciative article by Apollinaire in which he spoke of the 'fantaisie féerique' (fairylike fantasy) of his friend's verses.[1] And in an enigmatic sentence typical of his rich, metaphorical style he writes of Salmon: 'He has rounded off his lyricism with a touch of irony that if one were to change it into a flower would undoubtedly become a myosotis.'[2]

It was in part this irony that kept Salmon from plunging into the cubist fray. His irony and his caution. Having discovered Radiguet, he went on to criticize the young prodigy's 'abus des blancs,' the excessive sprinkling, that is, of meaningless blanks between lines and fragments to form what Salmon designates (perhaps ironically) the 'architecture typographique' of the poem. In *Carreaux* (1918) Salmon allowed himself some line play, but he was basically opposed to the experimental daring of the cubist poets, typographical and otherwise.

The excerpts printed above are from *Carreaux* (Tiles). The first passage contains the opening lines of *Prikaz*, an 'epic poem' commemorating the Russian revolution, with Salmon as an on-the-spot witness. The theme of the poem could be summed up, with apologies to Mme Roland, as follows: 'Oh innocence, what crimes are committed in thy name!' The poem is in vers libre. The apparently illogical juxtaposition in the penultimate stanza of the professor's voice and the cossack's voice could be cited as an example of cubist discontinuity.

Peindre (Painting) is a collection of verses inspired in part by Salmon's

Plate 15. *André Salmon*, portrait by Moïse Kissling. Copyright 1991, ARS, N.Y./ ADAGP.

1. Guillaume Apollinaire, 'André Salmon,' *Verse et Prose*, June–August 1908.

2. Guillaume Apollinaire, 'Critique littéraire,' in *Oeuvres complètes de Guillaume Apollinaire*, ed. Michel Décaudin, 4 vols. (Paris: Balland et Lecat, 1966), 4:828.

activities as an art critic for the daily press and author of *La Jeune Peinture française,* but mainly by Salmon the poet, who presents 'un monde récréé (a recreated world), the world of art, a world in which the good people exclaim: 'Il fait un temps de Tiepolo!' (What Tiepolo weather today!). Montmartre becomes a land of enchantment, and its inhabitants, poets and painters alike, chosen it seems more or less at random or because a name rhymes, act out their roles like marionettes. They are more than real in their unreality, somewhat like the faces that stare out from the artist groups of Marie Laurencin (see plate 9).

SELECTED BIBLIOGRAPHY

General Studies

Bertrand, Gérard. *L'Illustration de la poésie de l'époque du cubisme, 1909–1914*. Paris: Klincksieck, 1971.

Fauchereau, Serge. *La Révolution cubiste*. Paris: Denoël, 1982.

Fry, Edward F. *Cubism*. New York: McGraw Hill, 1966.

Guiney, Mortimer. *Cubisme et litterature*. Geneva: Georg, 1972.

Schwartz, Paul Waldo. *The Cubists*. London: Thames & Hudson, 1971.

Shattuck, Roger. *The Banquet Years*. New York: Harcourt Brace, 1958.

Stein, Donna. *Cubist Prints/Cubist Books*. New York: Franklin Furnace, 1983.

Wallen, Burr, and Donna Stein. *The Cubist Print*. Santa Barbara: University Art Museum, University of California, 1981.

Individual Poets

ALBERT-BIROT

Albert-Birot, Pierre. *Choix de textes*. Edited by Jean Follain. Collection Poètes d'aujourd'hui. Paris: Seghers, 1967.

——. *Poésie (1916–1924)*. Paris: Gallimard, 1967.

APOLLINAIRE

Apollinaire, Guillaume. *Alcools*. Translated by Anne Hyde Greet. Berkeley: University of California Press, 1965.

——. *Calligrammes: Poems of Peace and War (1913–1916) / Guillaume Apollinaire*. Translated by Anne Hyde Greet. Introduction and commentary by Anne Hyde Greet and S. I. Lockerbee. Berkeley and Los Angeles: University of California Press, 1980.

——. *Méditations esthétiques: Les Peintres cubistes*. Edited by L. C. Breunig and J.-Cl. Chevalier. Paris: Hermann, 1980.

——. *Oeuvres complètes de Guillaume Apollinaire*. Edited by Michel Décaudin. 4 vols. Paris: Balland et Lecat, 1966.

——. *Oeuvres poétiques de Guillaume Apollinaire*. Bibliothèque de la Pléïade. Paris: Gallimard, 1959. 2d ed. 1965.

——. *Selected Writings of Guillaume Apollinaire*. Translated with a critical introduction by Roger Shattuck. New York: New Directions, 1950.

Breunig, L. C. *Guillaume Apollinaire*. New York: Columbia University Press, 1969.

Greet, Anne Hyde. *Apollinaire et le livre de peintre–Bestiaire*. Paris: Minard, 1977.

Shattuck, Roger. 'Apollinaire's Great Wheel.' In *The Innocent Eye*. New York: Farrar, Straus, & Giroux, 1984.

Steegmuller, Francis. *Apollinaire: Poet among Painters*. New York: Farrar & Strauss, 1963.

CENDRARS

Cendrars, Blaise. *Du monde entier: Poésies complètes, 1912–1924*. Edited by Paul Morand. Collection Poésie. Paris: Gallimard, 1967.

——. *Poésies complètes de Blaise Cendrars*. Paris: Denoël, 1944.

——. *Selected Writings*. Edited by Walter Albert. New York: New Directions, 1966.

Bochner, Jay. *Blaise Cendrars: Discovery and Re-creation*. Toronto: University of Toronto Press, 1978.

Chefdor, Monique. *Blaise Cendrars*. Boston: Twayne, 1980.

COCTEAU

Cocteau, Jean. *Le Cap de Bonne-Espérance*. Collection Poésie. Paris: Gallimard, 1967.

——. *Poésie*. Paris: Gallimard, 1920.

Steegmuller, Francis. *Cocteau: A Biography*. Boston: Little, Brown, 1970.

DELAUNAY

Cohen, Arthur. *Sonia Delaunay*. New York: Harry Abrams, 1975.

Dorival, Bernard. *Sonia Delaunay: Sa vie, son oeuvre*. Paris: Damase, 1980.

DERMÉE

Dermée, Paul. *Spirales*. Paris: Birault, 1917.

——. In *Nord-Sud*, nos. 1–14 (March 1917–April 1918).

——. In *SIC*, nos. 12, 14–15, 19–20, 37–39, 42–43 (December 1916, February–March, July–August 1917, January–February, March–April 1919).

Décaudin, Michel. 'Cubisme littéraire: Le Cas Dermée.' In *Europe*, June–July 1982.

DRIEU LA ROCHELLE

Drieu La Rochelle, Pierre. *Écrits de jeunesse*. Paris: Gallimard, 1941.

Desanti, Dominique. *Drieu La Rochelle: Le seducteur mystifié*. Paris: Flammarion, 1978.

GARDELLE

Gardelle, Charlotte. In *SIC*, nos. 40–41, 44, 47–48 (February–April, June 1919).

HUIDOBRO

Huidobro, Vicente. *Obras completas*. Santiago: Editorial Andrés Bello, 1976. French texts remain in French.

———. *Poesía y prosa: Antología de Vicente Huidobro*. Aguilar: Juan Bravo, 1967.

———. *Selected Poetry*. Introduction and translations by David Guess. New York: New Directions, 1981.

de Costa, René. *Vicente Huidobro: The Careers of a Poet*. Oxford: Clarendon Press, 1984.

JACOB

Jacob, Max. *Le Cornet à dés*. Paris: Gallimard, 1945.

———. *The Dice Cup*. Edited by Michael Brownstein. New York: Sun, 1979.

———. *Le Laboratoire central*. Paris: Gallimard, 1960.

Kamber, Gerald. *Max Jacob and the Poetics of Cubism*. Baltimore: Johns Hopkins Press, 1971.

LAURENCIN

Laurencin, Marie [Louise Lalanne, pseud.]. *Le Carnet des nuits*. Geneva: Pierre Cailler, 1956.

Allard, Roger. *Marie Laurencin*. Paris: Nouvelle Revue Française, 1925.

OETTINGEN

Oettingen, Hélène d'. *Nord-Sud*, nos. 3, 6–11 (May, August–December 1917, January 1918). Reprinted in *Nord-Sud: Revue littéraire* (Paris: Jean-Michel Place, 1980).

———. In *SIC*, nos. 37–39, 45–54 (January–February, May–June, October–December 1919).

———. In *Les Soirées de Paris*, nos. 6, 18–19 (1912, 1913). Reprinted in *Les Soirées de Paris* (Geneva: Slatkine Reprints, 1971), vols. 1 and 2.

RADIGUET

Radiguet, Raymond. *Choix de textes*. Edited by David Noakes. Collection Poètes d'aujourd'hui. Paris: Seghers, 1968.

Crosland, Margaret. *Raymond Radiguet*. London: Owen, 1976.

REVERDY

Reverdy, Pierre. *Les Ardoises du toit*. In *Plupart du temps I (1915–1922)*. Collection Poésie. Paris: Gallimard, 1969.

———. *Le Gant de crin*. Paris: Librairie Plon, 1926.

———. *Nord-Sud, Self Defense et autres écrits sur l'art et la poésie (1917–1926)*. Edited by Etienne-Alain Hubert. Paris: Flammarion, 1975.

Greene, Robert W. 'Pierre Reverdy.' In *Six French Poets of Our Time*. Princeton: Princeton University Press, 1979.

Rizzuto, Anthony. *Style and Theme in Reverdy's 'Les Ardoises du toit.'* University: University of Alabama Press, 1971.

Rubin, William. *Picasso and Braque Pioneering Cubism.* New York: Museum of Modern Art, 1989.

SALMON

Salmon, André. *Carreaux.* Paris: Gallimard, 1928.

——. *Choix de textes.* Edited by Pierre Berger. Collection Poetes d'ajourd'hui. Paris: Seghers, 1956.

INDEX

Page numbers in italics refer to poems and art reproductions. Untitled poems, numbered poems, and poems entitled "Poem" are indexed by their first lines, which are enclosed in brackets.

"Académie Médrano" (Cendrars), *104*, 110

"[Ace of spades]" (Dermée), *149*, 159

"Adieu" (Reverdy), *280–81*

"Agrafes d'Argent" (Dermée), *144–47*

"[A Il y a]" (Oettingen), *244*

"L'Air" (Gardelle), *174–75*, 177

"Air" (Reverdy), *276–77*, 285

Albert-Birot, Pierre, xiv, xv, *1–18*, 19–21, 171, 265

Alcools (Apollinaire), xxiii, 71, 73, 265; etchings for, xxi, 305; lack of punctuation in, xix, 177

"A Linda" (Apollinaire), *24*, 70

Also Sprach Zarathustra (Nietzsche), 172

André Salmon (Kissling), *306*

Angiboult, François. *See* Oettingen, Hélène d'

Apelles, 71

Apollinaire, Guillaume, xiv, xv, xxiv, 69–79; as art critic, xvi, xvii, 69, 139, 226, 307; and Cendrars, 107, 109, 141; cubist collaborations of, xviii, xxi, xxiii, xxvii–xxviii, 110; on Gardelle, 177; influence of, xix, xviii, 19, 20, 159, 172, 196, 253, 265, 266; and Laurencin, 235–37; and d'Oettingen, 247; in others' poems, 6–9, 235; performances of works by, 129–30; poems by, *24–67*, 305; portraits of, xxi, *68, 69*

Apollinaire (Tamburi), *68*

"L'Après-midi d'un faune" (Mallarmé), 251

Archipenko, Aleksandr Porfiryevich, 109

Les Ardoises du toit (Reverdy), 283

Arnauld, Céline, 159

"[As de pique]" (Dermée), *148*, 159

Aujourd'hui (Cendrars), xvii

Auric, Georges, 8, 9

The Autobiography of Alice B. Toklas (Stein), 236

"Aux jeunes poètes" (Albert-Birot), 21

"Aveugle" (Huidobro), *182*, 195

"Balalaïka" (Albert-Birot), *10, 11*, 20

Le Bal du comte d'Orgel (Salmon), 265

Ballets Russes, 129

Baroness d'Oettingen (Survage), 252

The Baroness d'Oettingen with friends (De Chirico), *248*

Bateau-Lavoir (Montmartre area), xiv, xviii, xxv, 283, 305. *See also* Montmartre

Baudelaire, Charles, 75, 196

Beautés de 1918 (Dermée), 159

Bertin (singer), 8, 9

Bestiaire (Apollinaire), 237

"Blind" (Huidobro), *183*, 195

"[bluesky]" (Albert-Birot), *3*

"Bonds" (Apollinaire), *47–49*, 75

Le Bonnet d'âne (Radiguet), 266

A Book Concluding With as a Wife Has a Cow (Stein), xxi

Le Bourgeois gentilhomme (Molière), 71

Braque, Georges, xiii, xix, xv, xxv, 69, 110

"Cadran sans aiguilles" (Radiguet), *262*, 267

Calligrammes (Apollinaire), 75–77, 266, 267

calligrams (shaped poems), *62–67*, 77–79

"Cantor" (Apollinaire), 27, 71

Le Cap de Bonne-Espérance (Cocteau), *114– 27*, 131–32

The Cape of Good Hope (Cocteau), *115–27*, 131–32

Le Carnet des nuits (Laurencin), 237

Carreaux (Salmon), 307

La Cartelletre (Gris), xix, *xx*

Cendrars, Blaise, xiii, xiv, xv, 107–10, 172, 235, 266; cubist collaborations of, xvii, 110, 141–42; on Picasso, xvii; in poems, 8, 9, 141; poems by, *82–105*; publishing house of, 131

Cérusse, Jean. *See* Oettingen, Hélène d'

"[Ces pommes]" (Dermée), *154*

"Chantre" (Apollinaire), *26*, 71

"Le Cheval" (Laurencin), 232, 237

Chevaux de minuit (Oettingen), 253

"Chez Paul Guillaume" (Albert-Birot), *6–9*, 19

"Chronique des Marins Americains" (Albert-Birot), 19

"Chronique-Jazz" (Albert-Birot), 19

"[cielbleu]" (Albert-Birot), *2*

Cinq grandes odes (Claudel), 172

"[The City is free of sin]" (Albert-Birot), *5*

"Clameurs" (Oettingen), *242*, 249

Claudel, Paul, 171, 172

Cocteau, Jean, xiv, xxiv, 129–32, 172; cubist collaborations of, xvii, 110; poems by, *112–27*; self-portrait by, *128*

Coeur de chêne (Reverdy), xix

"[Coffee grinder]" (Dermée), *153*

Coleridge, Samuel Taylor, xxv

Colette, Sidonie-Gabrielle, 236

"Contrastes" (Cendrars), *92–97*, 110

"Le Coq et la Perle" (Jacob), *200–203*

Le Cornet à dés (Jacob), xv, 227

"Cortège" (Apollinaire), xxi, xxiii

"Un Coup de dés jamais n'abolira le hasard" (Mallarmé), xvi, 131

creationism, xv, 196

cubism: Apollinaire's contributions to, 69– 79; and art, xiii; characteristics of, xxiv– xxv, 226–27, 283–86; collaboration among artists, poets, and musicians in, xiii, xvii–xxviii, 69, 109–10, 129–31, 158,

159, 226, 249, 251, 253, 265; origins of
   term, xv–xvi; and poetry, xiii, xxiii–xxiv,
   226–27. *See also names of cubists*
cummings, e. e., xiii

dadaism, 20, 159, 237
Dante Alighieri, 285
Debussy, Claude, 6, 7
De Chirico, Giorgio, 248, 249
Delaunay, Robert, xiii, xxiv, xxv, 75, 76, 107,
   109, 139, 236
Delaunay-Terk, Sonia, xiv, xxiv, 76, 107–8,
   134–37, 139–42
Les Demoiselles d'Avignon (Picasso), 226,
   305
Denise (Radiguet), xix, 265
"Départ" (Reverdy), *274–75*, 285
"Departure" (Reverdy), *275*, 285
Derain, André, xvii, xviii, 69
Dermée, Paul, xiv, xxi, 157, 159, 283; art
   works by, *158;* cubist collaborations of,
   xvii, xxi, 158, 159; poems by, *144–55;* por-
   trait of, *156*
"Dernière Nouvelle" (Drieu La Rochelle).
   See "Rondeur"
Desanti, Dominique, 171
Descartes, René, 284
Deutsch, Babette, xxiii–xxiv
"Deux Poèmes" (Dermée), *152–55*
Le Diable au corps (Radiguet), 265

Diaghilev, Serge, 129
"Dimanche tranquille" (Gardelle), *174,* 178
Dix-neuf poèmes élastiques (Cendrars), 108–
   9
Donkey's bonnet (Radiguet), 266
Doucet, Jacques, 226
Drieu La Rochelle, Pierre, xiv, *162–69*, 171–
   72

Les Editions de la Sirène (publishing
   house), 131
"[un édredon rouge à la fenetre]" (Salmon),
   256, 265, 266
"Eiffel Tower" (Huidobro), *189–93*, 195, 196
Eluard, Paul, 285
L'Enchanteur pourrissant (Apollinaire), xviii,
   69
"L'Enfer" (Apollinaire), xxi
"En Forme de Cheval" (Apollinaire), *62,* 78
"L'Esprit Nouveau" (Apollinaire's slogan), 70
L'Esprit nouveau (periodical), 159
"[Est-ce un avion dans le ciel]" (Dermée),
   150–51

"Fairy Scene" (Cocteau), *113,* 130
"Féerie" (Cocteau), *112,* 130
Les Féeries (Salmon), 307
"Les Fenêtres" (Apollinaire), *50–52*
Férat, Serge Jastredzoff, *ii,* xvii, xxvii, 247,
   249

Le Festin d'Estope (review), 69

"Fête" (Apollinaire), *58–61, 76–77*

La Fin du monde (Cendrars), 110

"The Flower Pot" (Apollinaire), *66–67,* 78–79

Fond de Cantine (Drieu La Rochelle), 171–72

"Fountain" (Apollinaire), *65,* 78

Fuller, Loie, 235

futurism, 19, 70, 76

Gallien, Pierre, 156

Gardelle, Charlotte, xiv, *174–75,* 177–78

Garros, Roland, 131

Gauguin, Paul, 139

Gautier, Théophile, 75

"Générosité Espagnole" (Jacob), *206*

Gleizes, Albert, 236

Goldstein, Caroline, 159

Greet, Anne Hyde, 75

"Greetings, Blaise Cendrars" (Delaunay), *135–37*

Grey, Roch. *See* Oettingen, Hélène d'

Gris, Juan, 157; art works by, *158, 266, 282;* cubist collaborations of, xix, xvii, xxi, xxvii, 159, 226, 265; Kahnweiler on, 283

Group of Artists (Laurencin), *234*

Guillaume, Paul, 7, 8

"Hamac" (Cendrars), *98–101,* 109, 235, 266

"Hammock" (Cendrars), *99–101,* 109, 235, 266

"Handless Clock" (Radiguet), *263,* 267

"The Head" (Cendrars), *103*

"Hell" (Apollinaire), xxi

Homage to Bach (Braque), xxv

Homer, 285

"L'homme glisse" (Survage), *250,* 251

"Honneur de la Sardane et de la Tenora" (Jacob), *208–20,* 226

Horizon carré (Huidobro), 195, 267

"[horizon line]" (Radiguet), *259*

"Horse" (Apollinaire), *63,* 78

"The Horse" (Laurencin), *233*

d'Houville, Gérard, 236

Huidobro, Vicente, xiv, xv, *180–93,* 195–97, 249, 267

Husserl, Edmund, xvi

Illuminations (Rimbaud), xxv, 141

"Il pleut" (Apollinaire), 8, 9

"In Honor of the Sardana and the Tenora" (Jacob), *209–21,* 226

Interrogations (Drieu La Rochelle), 171

"In the Paul Guillaume Gallery" (Albert-Birot), *7–9,* 19

"Invitation au Voyage" (Jacob), *220–23,* 249

"[I play tennis with the shells]," *155*

"[Is it a plane in the sky]" (Dermée), *151*
"IV" (Albert-Birot), *2–3, 20*

Jacob, Max, xiii, xiv, xv, xxiv, xxv, 157, 225–27, 305; on Albert-Birot, 20–21; cubist collaborations of, xix, xvii, xviii, 110; influence of, 237, 249, 283; on d'Oettingen, 247; on Picasso, xvii, 225; poems by, *200–223*
J'ai tué (Cendrars), 110
Janssen, Camille. *See* Dermée, Paul
Jarry, Alfred, 69
"Jazz" (Drieu La Rochelle), 171
Jean Cocteau (Cocteau), *128*
"[Je joue à la paume avec les obus]" (Dermée), *154*
"Jet d'Eau" (Apollinaire), *64, 78*
La Jeune Peinture française (Salmon), xvi, 308

Kahnweiler, D. H., xix, xviii, 69, 226, 265, 283
"Kilima-N'Djaro" (Oettingen), *240–42,* 249
Kostrowitsky, Guillaume de. *See* Apollinaire, Guillaume

Le Laboratoire central (Jacob), xxiv
Laboureur, Allard, xvii
Lagut, Irène, *77,* 78
Lalanne, Louise (pseud.), 236, 237

"Laminated Memories (poster-poem)" (Albert-Birot), *13*
Laurencin, Marie, xiv, 235–37; art works by, *234,* 308; poems by, *230–33*
Laurens, Henri, xix, xvii, 159, 265
Le Fauconnier, Henri, 236
Legér, Fernan, xiii, xix, 110, 236
Lejeune, Emile, 109
"Lettre-Océan" (Apollinaire), 77
Liebig, Justus, 109
"Liens" (Apollinaire), *46–49,* 75, 267
"[Ligne d'horizon]" (Radiguet), *258,* 266–67
L'Intransigeant (newspaper), 69
"Little Poem" (Jacob), xxv, *205*
Le Livre (Férat), *ii,* xxvii
livres d'artistes, xvii–xix, xxi–xxii
livres de peintres, xvii–xix, xxi–xxii
La Lucarne oval (Reverdy), 196, 283
"Lundi rue Christine" (Apollinaire), *54–58,* 75, 76, 78
Lunes en papier (Malraux), xix

"Ma Danse" (Cendrars), *96–99,* 109
Mallarmé, Stéphane, xv–xvi, xviii, 131, 157, 251, 284
Malraux, André, xix, 131
Les Mamelles de Tirésias (Apollinaire), 129–30
Manet, Édouard, xviii
Manolo, xix

"Map" (Radiguet), *261, 266, 267*

Marcoussis, Louis, xvii, xxi, xxiii, 159, *304, 305*

Les Marges, 236

Massine, Léonide, 129

"Matin" (Huidobro), *186*, 196–97

Matisse, Henri, xv

Matorel, Victor, 226

Mayakovsky, V. V., 139

"Medrano Academy" (Cendrars), *105*, 110

métèques, xiii

Metzinger, Jean, 69, 236

"Midnight" (Huidobro), *185*, 195

"Minuit" (Huidobro), *184*, 195

modernism, 74

Modigliani, Amedeo, 247

Molière, 71

Molina da Silva, Linda, 70

"Monday rue Christine" (Apollinaire), *55–59*, 75, 76, 78

Montfort, Eugène, 236

Montjoie (avant-garde magazine), 70

Montmartre, xxvii, 157, 308. *See also* Bateau-Lavoir

Montparnasse, xxvii, 109, 131, 247

La Montre (Gris), xxi, *xxii*, 266

"Morning" (Huidobro), *187*, 196–97

"[Moulin à café]" (Dermée), *152*

Muse Inspiring the Poet (Rousseau), xiv, 236

"My Dance" (Cendrars), *97–99*, 109

Ne coupez pas Mademoiselle ou Les Erreurs des P.T.T. (Jacob), xix

neo-Symbolism, 69

"new aesthetic," 157

"New Song" (Huidobro), *181*, 195

Nietzsche, Friedrich, 171, 172

Nijinksy, V. F., 129

Noailles, Countess de, 236

Nord-Sud (cubist review), xiv, 157, 159, 195, 249, 283

"Nouvelle Chanson" (Huidobro), *180*, 195

nunism, xv, 19, 21

L'Ode à Picasso (Cocteau), 131, 172

Oedipus Rex (Cocteau-Stravinsky oratorio), 132

d'Oettingen, Hélène, xiv, xvii, xxiii, 247, 249, 251, 253; poems by, *240–45*; portraits of, *248, 252*, 253

"Les Oiseaux" (Laurencin), 237

"On the Threshold" (Reverdy), *273*, 284

Orloff, Justman, xvii

orphism, 70, 139

Ortiz, 247

"Outcries" (Oettingen), *243*, 249

painted poems, 197

Painting (Salmon), *295–303*, 307–8

Le Panama ou les Aventures des mes sept oncles (Cendrars), *91*, 108, 131

Papier collé (Dermée and Gris), *158*, 159
Les Pâques à New York (Cendrars), 107, 139
Parade (ballet), 129–30
"Paradis (poème-pancarte)" (Albert-Birot), *14*
"Paradise (placard-poem)" (Albert-Birot), *15*
Paris-Journal (newspaper), 69
Pascal, Blaise, 131
Paul Dermée (Gallien), *156*
"Peaceful Sunday" (Gardelle), *175*, 178
Pegasus, 78
Peindre (Salmon), *294–303*, 307–8
Les Peintres cubistes (Apollinaire), xvii, 71, 76, 236
Les Pélicans (Radiguet), xix, 265
Petit Bestiaire (Laurencin), 237
"Petit Poème" (Jacob), xxv, *204*
"Les Phares" (Baudelaire), 75
Picabia, Francis, 237
Picasso, Pablo, xv, xxv, 110, 307; cubist collaborations of, xvii, xviii, 129–31, 226, 253; on cubist poetry, xxiv; friends of, xiii, xiv, 235, 247, 305; poets on, xvi–xvii, 69, 110, 225–26; portraits of, 249
Le Piège de Méduse (Satie), xix
Pierre Reverdy (Gris), *282*
Pieux, Léonard. *See* Oettingen, Hélène d'
"Plan" (Radiguet), *260*, 266, 267
plastic poetry, 284
Pliny, 71

"Pluie" (Gardelle), *174*
La Plume, 69
poème-affiche, *12–13*, 19
poème-conversation, 19, 76, 78
"Poème lu au mariage d'André Salmon" (Apollinaire), xxiii, 305
poème-pancarte, *14–17*, 19
poème-promenade, 19, 73
Poèmes (Salmon), 307
"Poèmes à crier et à danser" (Albert-Birot), 20
"Poem read at the marriage of André Salmon" (Apollinaire), xxiii, 305
"Poems" (Gardelle), 178
"Poems for screaming and dancing" (Albert-Birot), 20
Poésie, 1916–1924 (Albert-Birot), 21
"la poésie plastique," 284
poet-critics, xvi
Poetry Handbook (Deutsch), xxiii–xxiv
Poiret, Paul, 171
"Poste" (Reverdy), *278–79*, 285
Pound, Ezra, xiii
"Le Présent" (Laurencin), *230*, 236
Prikaz (Salmon), *288–93*, 307
"Prose du Transsibérien et de la petite Jeanne de France" (Cendrars), *82–89*, 107–8, 141
Protogenes, 71

"Quand le symbolisme fut mort" (Dermée), 157

"[Quel est cet enfant blond qui court en riant après ses billes de couleurs]?" (Albert-Birot), *4*

Racine, Jean, 284
Radiguet, Raymond, xiv, xix, *256–63*, 265–67, 307
"Rain" (Gardelle), *175*
Rajky, Raimon. *See* Salmon, André
"[a red eiderdown at the window]" (Radiguet), *257*
Reverdy, Pierre, xiii, xiv, xxiv, 157, 195, 196, 249, 283–86; cubist collaborations of, xix, 110; on Picasso, xvii; poems by, *270–81*; portrait of, *282*
"Revolution" (Drieu La Rochelle), 171
Rimbaud, Arthur, xxv, 139, 141, 157, 171, 253, 265
"Road" (Reverdy), *271*, 284–86
Romain, xv
"Rondeur" (Drieu La Rochelle), *166–69*, 171, 172
Roof slates (Reverdy), 283
"The Rooster and the Pearl" (Jacob), *201–3*
"Roundness" (Drieu La Rochelle), *166–69*, 171, 172
Rousseau, Henri (Le Douanier), xiv, 236, 249
"Route" (Reverdy), *270*, 284–86
Russian Revolution, 307

Le Sacre du Printemps (Stravinsky), 129
Sagot, Clovis, 235
Sailor in a Bar (Marcoussis), *304*
Saint Matorel trilogy (Jacob), xviii, 226
La Salle Huyghens gallery, 109
Salmon, André, xiv, 265, 305–8; and Apollinaire, xxiii, 69; cubist collaborations of, xvii, 110; on Picasso, xvi–xvii; poems by, *288–303*; portrait of, *306*
Salon d'Automne (1911), xiv, 70, 177
Salon des Indépendants, 69, 70, 235, 236
"Salut, Blaise Cendrars" (Delaunay), *134–37*
Satie, Erik, xix, 8, 9, 109, 129–30
Saurat, Henriette, 8, 9
Sauser, Frédéric. *See* Cendrars, Blaise
"Secteur américain" (Drieu La Rochelle), 171
Section d'Or exhibit (1912), 70
shaped poems (calligrammes), *62–67*, 77–79, 266, 267
Shattuck, Roger, 77
SIC (cubist review), xiv, 19, 157, 171, 177, 249, 265, 266
"Silver Clasps" (Dermée), *145–47*
"simultanism," xiv, xxiv–xxv, 107–9
Les Six, 109–10
Les Soirées de Paris (avant-garde magazine), xiv, 70, 72, 73, 108, 247, 249, 266
"Le soleil est dans l'escalier (poème-pancarte)" (Albert-Birot), *16*
Soupault, Philippe, 139

"Souvenirs laminés (poème-affiche)" (Albert-Birot), *12*

"Spanish Generosity" (Jacob), *207*

Spectre de la Rose (ballet), 129

Spirales (Dermée), 159

Stein, Gertrude, xiii, xxi, 225, 236, 247

Stein, Leo, 225

Steinlen, Théophile-Alexandre, 225

Stravinsky, Igor, 129, 132

Der Sturm (avant-garde magazine), 70

"The sun is in the staircase (placard-poem)" (Albert-Birot), *17*

"Sur le seuil" (Reverdy), 272, 284

surrealism, 285

Survage, Léopold, xvii, xxiii, 77–78, 247, 249, 251, 253; art works by, *250, 252*

Symbolism, xxv, 69, 157, 305

Tamburi, Orfeo, 68

"Tennis" (Drieu La Rochelle), *162–65,* 172

"La Tête" (Cendrars), *102,* 109

"[These apples]" (Dermée), *155*

391 (dadaist magazine), 237

"Le Tigre" (Laurencin), *232–33,* 237

"[To Ilya]" (Oettingen), *245*

"To Linda" (Apollinaire), *25,* 70

"To the young poets" (Albert-Birot), *21*

Toulouse-Lautrec, Henri de, 225

"Tour Eiffel" (Huidobro), *188–93,* 195, 196

Tout à coup (Huidobro), 197

Trente et un poèmes des poche (Albert-Birot), 19

"T.S.F." (Drieu La Rochelle), 171

"Two Poems" (Dermée), *153–55*

Uhde, Wilhelm, 139

unanimism, xv

"Usine" (Drieu La Rochelle), 171

Van Dongen, Kees, 177

Van Gogh, Vincent, 139

"Vase" (Apollinaire), *66–67, 78–79*

Vauxcelles, Louis, xv, xvi

"Vengeance" (Drieu La Rochelle), 171

"Vernissages" (Albert-Birot), 19

Vico, Giambattista, xvii

"[La ville est sans péché]" (Albert-Birot), *4*

Le Volant d'Artimon (Dermée), 159

Vollard's gallery, 225

"Le Voyageur" (Apollinaire), *26–31,* 71–73, 266

Les Voyelles de Rimbaud (R. Delaunay), xxv, *xxvi,* 139

"Voyelles" (Rimbaud), xxv, 139

Weill, Berthe, 177

"[Who is that blond child laughing as he runs after his colored marbles?]" (Albert-Birot), *5*

Williams, William Carlos, xiii

"Windows" (Apollinaire), *51–53*, 75–76

"Window" series (R. Delaunay), 75, 109

World War I, xiii, 171, 249; and cubism, xxvii, 70, 76–77, 110, 131

World War II, 171, 227

"XV" (Albert-Birot), *4, 5, 20*

"XVII" (Albert-Birot), *4, 5,* 20

Zdanevitch, Ilya ("Iliazd"), 253

"Le Zèbre" (Laurencin), *232–33*

Zenith (S. Delaunay), *134, 135, 140,* 141–42

"Zone" (Apollinaire), xxiv, *32–47,* 73–75, 107, 196, 266